WHO SAID A *Woman* CAN'T PREACH

Breaking the mold and upsetting the establishment with the ungarnished truth

Leander Hicks

MW01247715

WHO SAID A *Woman* CAN'T PREACH

Breaking the mold and upsetting the establishment with the ungarnished truth

Leander Hicks

T&J PUBLISHERS

Printed in the United States of America by
T&J Publishers (Atlanta, GA.)
www.TandJPublishers.com

© Copyright 2024 by Leander Hicks

All rights reserved. This book or parts thereof may not be reproduced in any form, stored in a retrieval system, or transmitted in any form by any means-electronic, mechanical, photocopy, recording, or otherwise-without prior written permission of the author, except as provided by United States of America copyright law.

Cover Design by Timothy Flemming, Jr.
(T&J Publishers)
Book Format/Layout by Timothy Flemming, Jr.

ISBN: 979-8-3303-2520-7

To contact the author, go to:

Email: Abrilliantgem@aol.com

DEDICATIONS

This book is dedicated to the memory of my mother, Ms. Mattie Lue T. H. Thigpen. As you may or may not know she was considered illiterate. Illiterate is defined as *a person being uneducated*. She was inadequate in book knowledge, but every opportunity presented her she eagerly turned into a capability.

Her inability to read and speak fluent grammar was embarrassing for me early on. Yes, I was ashamed of my mother's literacy problem. But Mom had no shame. Her total dependence was on the Lord. He led and guided her into all truth. Mom had phenomenal wisdom that surpassed all book knowledge.

My mom constantly reminded me that I was not responsible for how people treated me; I am, however, responsible for how I treat people. I now understand what she meant. It does not matter if a person is being fair or unfair; my responsibility is to God. My mom's very existence exemplified the love of God. That kind of love can only come from God.

I also dedicate this book to my daughter who went to be with the Lord in Heaven in 2022, Yolanda A. Grubbs. I love you so much and cannot wait to be reunited with you again. Thank you for all of your love, encouragement and support, and being an awesome gift in my life.

The ELA teachers at the school where I work for 5 years have been very instrumental in my writing skills.

Yolanda Grubbs
— with **Yolanda Grubbs**.

JUN 2, 2020

18

PhotoGrid

Like   Commer

TABLE OF CONTENTS

Foreword

You're probably asking yourselves, *why is this author qualified to pen this book?* Better yet, *how will her experiences help me in life and ministry?* If you will allow me a few minutes, I can stir-up the seasoning of curiosity and hesitation that will result into an infatuation to move forward. Knowing the author over 30 years, it's not uncommon for her to show the compassion and zeal to lift someone's spirit or even minister to the loveless, lost and left out. Her discernment to intercede in prayer and the timeliness and boldness to seek God in all things, is overwhelming.

    Looking forward into the Chapters to come, she displays the pitfalls of life that so easily besets us on our journey as disciples for Christ. I have personally received guidance and motivation from her during some of my own challenges and dark moments. This is all factual and not fiction. The following is my brief prelude and observation of the author's directives.

In Chapter One, Unlearning -"Forgetting What You Know", is a reflection of becoming stagnant in spirit (Isaiah 55:6-7). We get to the point of believing we know-it-all rather than seeking God to know what He's doing in our lives (Matthew 4:19).

In Chapter Two, Leaving the Pew – "Ministry is Only the Beginning", here we are girded up and prepared to preach the gospel to all nations (Mark 16:15). Yet faced with obstacles, criticism, mocked or misunderstood,remember as a servant for the Lord, we must be of good courage. Those spiritual chains that seem to bind us only represent enduring strength and stability (Psalm 116.16a).

In Chapter Three, A Wounded Soul – "Dealing with Forgiveness and Religious Bondage." So many of us have experienced the pain inflicted from someone you loved or have fellowshipped with in the church. The Word of God says forgive them (Matthew 6:14-15); but if you do not forgive, our Father in Heaven will NOT forgive us. The author can attest this can be a very difficult task to do, but trusting in God will make this challenge your "come-back." (See Galatians 5:1 and John 8:36.)

Chapter Four, Supernatural Provision – "God's Desire to Lead Us into the Blessing He Has Prepared for Us Only Through Hearing His Voice." (John 10:27-28) Man can make you several offers, but it is only God - that will keep you and fulfill every promise.

Lastly, Chapter Five – "Staying Faithful to God." (Romans 10:17, John 8:32 and Philippians 4:11-13) Learn the secret of being content. Evangelist Leander Hicks, remain this faithful and diligent Woman of God! Be steadfast, unmovable, always abounding in the work of the Lord; forasmuch as ye know that your labor is not in vain in the Lord. "WHO SAID A WOMAN CAN'T PREACH?" Obviously, anyone that does not know who God is! The 28th Chapter of ACTS reads: "whom the Lord choses, He calls and qualifies!"

Linda Samuel-Brown
Saint Paul Baptist Church of Oxnard, CA. | Ministry Leadership (>65 yrs.)
United States Navy | Program Analyst (>50 yrs.)

Introduction

I T WAS HOLY WEEK. THIS IS A TIME OF celebration for Christian, a time when we remember and reflect on the final days of Christ leading up to His death and resurrection. Of course, in those final days leading up to His crucifixion, Jesus left final instructions to His disciples, He ate His last supper with them in what is famously called The Upper Room, and agonized in the Garden of Gethsemane over the suffering He was about to experience. And who wouldn't agonize over the thought of such suffering? Crucifixion was a horrible death, one that was excruciatingly painful. He was about to hang on a cross for several hours, fighting for each breath as His chest collapsed over His diaphragm, cutting off His oxygen; His hands and feet being ripped by the long, spiked nails holding them in place as the weight of His body pulled Him down. And this is what happened after the scourging He endured at the hands of the Roman soldiers where they whipped the flesh off

His back using a flagrum, which was a whip consisting of a rope with metal balls, bones, and metal spikes. That alone should have killed Him, but He endured.

The celebration is over Christ's resurrection; that He went through Hell on earth just to take mankind's punishment for sin on the cross, but then He rose from the grave as prophesied in the Old Testament, signifying that He gained power over death and the grave, and is hence, a living Savior.

Holy Week is observed by every Christian denomination. That week, I was sitting in church at six o'clock on a Thursday morning, preparing for the worship service when I heard the voice of God. What He spoke into my spirit produced enough confusion and anxiety in me to almost make me sweat drops of blood. He told me something preposterous, something unthinkable, something unimaginable, something utterly despicable and unacceptable at the time. He spoke these exact words in my spirit:

I called you from your mother's womb.

I knew exactly what those words meant, as the Holy Spirit further impressed on my heart that I was called by God to preach the Gospel. Now, this might not sound like much to some people today in our progressive society, but this was 1987. Back then, women preachers were virtually unheard of, especially in the Baptist Church, which I was a part of. Me? Preaching? That was unthinkable. And yet, that's exactly what God spoke into my spirit that morning.

I was arrested by those words. I was suspended in disbelief, and yet, I was curious. It dawned on me that those words were also in the Bible. So I began flipping through the pages of my Bible to find the scripture, not even caring about what was going on during service. Interestingly enough, that verse found me because when I opened my Bible, it landed on the exact page where the verse was. It was Jeremiah 1:5—

> "Before I formed you in the belly, I knew you; and before thou came forth out of the womb I sanctified you, and I ordained thee a prophet unto the nations."

Some Bible scholars say Jeremiah was around seventeen-years old when God spoke those words to him; others claim he was around twenty. In either case, Jeremiah was the youngest prophet in Israelite history. What he did had never been done before. He set a new precedent and did the unthinkable. He didn't fit the mold of the traditional prophet. He didn't look the part. Most considered him too young to be a prophet. They said he was just a child—he even called himself that. Jeremiah's retort to God was, "But I'm just a child. I'm just a kid. No one's going to take me seriously. No one is going to listen to me."

God's response to Jeremiah's quip was this: "Say not, 'I'm just a child.'"

Like Jeremiah, I had an excuse, a legitimate one.

WHO SAID A WOMAN CAN'T PREACH?

In my church, in my Christian community, there had never been a woman preacher. And I certainly wasn't planning on breaking the mold, disrupting the tradition. We, women, were allowed to cook the food and bake the cakes and pies for homecoming services. We were allowed to serve in various roles: on the outreach teams, the missions teams, teach Sunday School, even teach the youth, but be it far from us to think we'd ever be accepted as licensed and ordained preachers and even pastors, bishops and apostles, which are higher ranks in the church.

And yet, that's what God was calling me to. Oh, boy!

*

Almost everyone God calls has an excuse why they can't do what God is telling them to do. I mean, Moses complained that he had a speech impediment. Jeremiah, as stated, complained about his age. David was overlooked because of his size and lack of decorum—he was simply a shepherd boy, hanging out with a bunch of stinking sheep; not considered kingly material. Even Israel's first king, Saul, saw himself as inadequate. Oftentimes, when God calls us, we're not ready—or at least, we don't feel ready. In the midst of the call, we're still dealing with mental, emotional and spiritual issues. We're still wrestling with doubts and fears, and even psychological and emotional hangups. We're battling staggering mountains of debt and even dealing with legal problems, health problems, family turmoil, abusive situa-

INTRODUCTION

tions, and more. I wish God's calling would come at a perfect time, at a time when we didn't have any issues to deal with and problems that hammered our self-esteems and made us feel unqualified. I wish He didn't call us when we were still wrestling with addictions and sins. That would be great. But that's not how God works. He doesn't wait until life is perfect to call us. He doesn't wait until we've gotten all of our ducks in a row and settled all of our personal affairs first. What He does is call us when we're in the midst of life, when we're not ready. I believe He does this because He doesn't want us to feel qualified and worthy. Think about it: Everything God does in and through us is the result of His power, not our ability; and He does it this way so that only He can get the glory. We'll never be able to take the credit for any of the things He does in us and through us. It's not our righteousness, our works, our smarts, our wits; it's His goodness, power, mercy and love that's working through us. We're just instruments, conduits through which His power flows. We're just messengers. We're not the message, the Savior, the healer, the deliverer. We just tell people about the healer, deliverer, Savior: Jesus.

Furthermore, God has a tendency of showing man who's really in charge. So when we get the big-head and think we're the ones running the show and setting the rules, that's when God will change things up and do something that's never been done before. He'll call a teenager and make him a prophet in a culture that didn't accept teenagers as prophets and rabbis, He'll call an outsider (Ruth) and raise her up to be the matriarch of the messianic bloodline, He'll call a woman (Deborah) to lead the Israelite army during a time of war and make her a judge over His people, He'll even call a murderer and persecutor of Christians and make him the greatest Christian evangelist to ever walk the face of the earth.

The Bible says,

> "Instead, God chose things the world considers foolish in order to shame those who think they are wise. And he chose things that are powerless to shame those who are powerful." (1 Corinthians 1:27, NLT)

God enjoys using people others have written off. He enjoys calling the very people we think don't deserve to be called. He enjoys blessing us through people we don't expect Him to use. He does crazy things sometimes. Things that baffle us. Things that leave us scratching our heads and wondering, "What just happened?" Just when we think we have God all figured out, He changes the game and does something different, something strange, something new. All we can do is follow God; we can't walk ahead of Him and predict what He's going to do.

And no one, myself included, could have predicted that He'd call me, a woman, into the ministry in one of the strictest denominations, the Baptist Church.

The calling of God on my life was about to take me on a journey I'd never expected. God was about to reveal His power to me in extraordinary ways and do the impossible in my life. This would also be a time that would cost me dearly and pull on me in ways I never imagined. Just because you're called, that doesn't mean the road is going to be smooth—I'm here to tell you, it won't be. It's going to contain bumps and potholes; it's going to bend and turn in unexpected ways; it's going to test your patience and endurance. But if you stick with God and stick to the word He's given you, you will experience unimaginable blessings and reaps the rewards of your labor.

If you know—or at least, believe—you're called, you'll want to pay very close attention to the content in the next chapter (and the rest of the book for that matter). Your success in God's calling will depend on it.

WHO SAID A WOMAN CAN'T PREACH?

Chapter 1

UNLEARNING

I GREW UP IN CHURCH. I REMEMBER LONG DAYS IN a hot sanctuary, everyone sweating while fanning themselves with whatever they could find. I remember wooden pews that tended to make us uncomfortable after a few minutes of sitting on them. The women would often get to dancing during service, and the men would lift their hands and shout. The preacher would be drenched in sweat as he stood behind the wooden podium and thundered the word of the Lord from the pulpit. During these service, I'd made a subtle observation—I'm sure everyone did, one no one mentioned out loud and dared make a fuss about: the other chairs in the pulpit would be filled with nothing but men. The only time we heard a woman's voice during service was when the choir was up.

The scary thing about tradition is that it often lacks sense and reason. Basically, we do things without ever questioning why we do them, and we fail to question how and why the tradition began in the first place. When we slip into a mold of tradition, we stop asking questions and simply accept what is; we stop being curious, and we become blind devotees to things that often make no sense and oftentimes conflict with the word of God.

Now, we all have traditions. We grow up with them. We live with them. At home, we see them played out in the household. For example, we eat turkey during Thanksgiving. We wrap gifts and place them under trees during Christmas and make the kids go to bed early, even frightening them by telling them, "Santa Claus will spit in your eyes if you stay awake on Christmas Eve." Some of us eat fried fish every Friday as if that day had been designated The Official Fried Fish Day by the government. Some of us attend weekly football games and/or basketball games as a tradition, especially at our alma maters.

We automate our lives using routines. We like to set our daily lives on a schedule so that we know what comes next, and what we'll do next. We don't like surprises; they create anxiety and make us feel like we're not in control of the day. So traditions give us something to look forward to, which isn't such a bad thing.

However, traditions can be stifling. They can prevent us from following God who is as unpredictable as the weather at times. He wants us to flow with Him, not try to predict and control Him. And that is what tradition cannot do: it cannot flow with God; it is about man's control; it's about feeling secure in that everything is going according to our plans. But to follow God, you must forget your plans. You must forget about your schedule, your calendar, your five-year and ten-year plan, your preconceived notions and ideas of how things are supposed to be and supposed to go. Jesus put it this way:

> "Then said Jesus unto his disciples, If any man will come after me, let him deny himself, and take up his cross, and follow me" (Matthew 16:24).

And if that wasn't assuring enough for you, try this one:

> "Whoever finds their life will lose it, and whoever loses their life for my sake will find it." (Matthew 10:39, NIV)

Denying ourselves, losing sight of our plans, and learning how to hear and follow God is the crux of the Christian faith. Christianity is not about rituals, symbols and traditions. To tell you the truth, it's not even about all of the sacraments we hold near and dear such as water baptism and communion. The Bible doesn't tell us we'll be saved if we get water baptized and take communion. The thief on the cross next to Jesus had time to do neither, and yet, he became a Believer the second he said, "Lord, when you enter into your kingdom, remember me!" Jesus immediately responded to him, saying,

"This day, you will be with me in paradise" (Luke 23:43).

Jesus didn't yell back and say, "Okay, let's do this: first, we'll climb down from these crosses, then we'll find the closest river or lake where I'll water baptized you and give you communion, and then we'll climb back onto these crosses and die, and then you'll be with me in paradise!" Jesus didn't even tell him to confess all of his sins and make amends with all of those he'd wronged first. Jesus didn't mention to him anything about works and deeds; He just acknowledged and accepted that man's profession of faith right there on the spot. No rituals, no process of time, and no sacraments needed; just faith.

We've overcomplicated salvation and the Gospel message with our traditions. And it's because of this people are experiencing religion rather than salvation—and there's a difference between the two. In short, we have a bunch of people who're religious but not saved.

Now, don't get me wrong, I'm not saying there's something wrong with water baptism and communion. I'm certainly not implying that these are useless activities. I believe they are important parts of our faith as Christians. They are symbolic acts that let the world know who we serve and to whom we belong. But aside from that, the only thing one must do to be saved is believe on the name of Jesus and accept salvation by faith. That's it! You can make it into Heaven without all of that other stuff. I mean, that is what Romans 10:9-10 declares:

"If you declare with your mouth, 'Jesus is Lord,'

and believe in your heart that God raised him from the dead, you will be saved. For it is with your heart that you believe and are justified, and it is with your mouth that you profess your faith and are saved." (NIV)

We must all learn of Christ in order to grow in our faith, but for many of us, becoming effective as Believers and walking in God's will for our lives entails unlearning many of the things we've been taught through religion. Yes, we must spend time unlearning religion and learning faith. That's hard to do. Trust me, I know. And the older you get and the longer you remain trapped in religion, the harder it is to break free from religious bondage.

That's what religion is basically: bondage.

After God called me into the ministry, I knew I had to gear up for a fight. I realized I had to come armed with information and truth. So I took some time and educated myself on the history of the Baptist Church in order to get a better understanding of its traditions. What I really wanted to know was why women preachers were prohibited.

In my research, I learned the Baptists is one of the largest denominations, reaching into almost every continent. Statistics suggested that Baptists are believed to be the largest group of denominational born-again Christians in the United States of America. The doctrine for most Baptist is evangelical—the term "evangelical" pertains to certain movements in the Protestant churches in the eighteenth and nineteenth centuries that stress the importance of personal experience of guilt for sin and of reconciliation to God through Christ. However, their beliefs can vary due to congregational governance system. There is a widespread difference among their doctrinal issues.

In Christianity, there are multiple denominations having different beliefs concerning specific topics. However, the one thing every Christian denomination should agree on is the exclusivity of Christ: that there's only one Savior, Jesus, and only through Him can man find salvation, redemption, forgiveness of sins, and obtain access into the Kingdom of Heaven. We should also agree on certain fundamental dogmas within the Christian faith such as Jesus being born of a virgin, dying on the cross and rising from the grave on the third day, and the reality of Heaven and a Hell, angels and demons.

Aside from these core beliefs, denominations can argue with each other over other things like the type of baptism we should receive (submerged or sprinkled), the nature of the Trinity, certain eschatological events (whether you believe in the rapture of the church, and if so, whether you're a pre-tribulation or post-tribulation proponent); Dominion theology, Calvinism, Replacement Theology, whether we should have church on Saturday or Sunday, whether or not the charismatic gifts such as prophecy and divine healing still apply today, whether or not women and children can preach, and even the importance and relevance of the five-fold ministry consisting of prophets, apostles, teachers, pastors and evangelists.

Now, the Baptist denomination as a whole doesn't believe in the charismatic gifts of the Holy Spirit, they don't accept several of the offices of the five-fold ministry—they don't acknowledge the office of the prophet, nor do they use the titles of bishop, apostle, and elder—and they certainly don't believe in women preachers. Ironically, the bulk of the things the Baptist denomination denounces are the things God was calling me to. He wasn't just calling me to the ministry, He was also calling me to the anointing—to walk in the power of the Holy Spirit and operate in spiritual gifts such as speaking in tongues, laying hands on the sick and believing for miracles, prophesying and giving words of knowledge, etc. What God was doing in my life was breaking the mold of what I'd come to believe was acceptable and normal for a Believer. He was snatching me out of bondage by calling me to greater. He was dealing with me about everything I'd previously come to believe.

One thing I do love about the Baptist denomination is their love for foundational teaching. They believe in solid, Bible teaching. They specialize in Sunday School. It's just that they tend to skip over the parts of the Bible that they don't fully understand (one being the spiritual gifts). Still, the Baptist Church will lay a firm foundation in you when it comes to the basics of the Christian faith. And to that point, you don't need to speak in tongues to be saved. However, you do need the gift of tongues among other gifts in order to be effective witnesses for Christ. In Acts 1:8, Jesus told His disciples,

"But you will receive power when the Holy Spirit comes upon you. And you will be my witnesses, telling people about me everywhere—in Jerusalem, throughout Judea, in Samaria, and to the ends of the earth" (NLT). And we know what happened when the Holy Spirit came upon the disciples on the Day of Pentecost. The Bible shares what happened in great detail:

> "When the day of Pentecost came, they were all together in one place. Suddenly a sound like the blowing of a violent wind came from heaven and filled the whole house where they were sitting. They saw what seemed to be tongues of fire that separated and came to rest on each of them. All of them were filled with the Holy Spirit and began to speak in other tongues[a] as the Spirit enabled them." (Acts 2:1-4, NIV)

Those men began speaking in tongues and operating under the supernatural power of the Holy Spirit. It was that power that enabled them to preach to the very Jews they were hiding from and add over three-thousand souls to the church in one day (yes, over three-thousand Jews gave their lives to Christ that day). If the disciples had not been filled with the Holy Spirit that day, they would not have impacted the world for Christ that day—or any other day.

People don't want to simply read and hear about the sick being healed and the dead being raised; they want to see it with their own eyes. People don't want to simply talk about miracles; they want to experience them. And God is eager to show off His miraculous power, but He needs Believers who're willing to allow Him to fill them with this power. Sadly, that's where many Baptist draw the line. They'll tell God no in a heartbeat. They shun the things they don't understand, and denounce these as obsolete, even heretical and unnecessary.

Concerning the topic of women preachers, in the early 1970s, Baptist groups were defining what they deemed "traditional gender roles". This was around the same time that the Women's Liberation Movements was evolving. The rules and regulations created were designed to specifically prevent women from becoming pastors of Baptist congregations. The Baptists chose to allow women to serve in the ministry on Baptist boards, writer pools, mission teams, faculties and as professional staff, but they were not eligible for pastorship. They made it clear to women what their "place" was at the time. They later went on to define the pastoral office as being exclusively the domain of males.

The scripture they use to draw this conclusion is found in 1 Timothy 2:11-12, which says, "Let the woman learn in silence with all subjection. But I suffer not a woman to teach, nor to usurp authority over the man, but to be in silence." At a cursory glance, it appears as if the Apostle Paul was prohibiting all women from teaching and preaching in the church; however, when you take a deeper look, you'll discover that's not what Paul was saying.

First, let's examine whether or not the Apostle Paul was opposed to women serving in ministry as teachers and preachers. It doesn't take long for us to come to the conclusion that Paul was not opposed to women teaching, preaching, prophesying, and even pastoring. He wasn't opposed to women operating in leadership roles—he commended several women who served in such roles. Perhaps the most famous among them was Phoebe, who Paul mentioned in Romans 16:1-2. He trusted her to deliver his letter to the Christians in Rome.

Paul called Phoebe as diakonos, which is the Greek word for "deacon". A deacon is a Christian designated to serve as an overseer for the church. So I find it interesting that many church leaders will ignore the importance of Paul's acknowledgment of Phoebe and continue to insist that Paul neither wanted nor allowed women to have in authority in the church.

The Apostle Paul told the church to cooperate with Phoebe. He instructed them to "assist" her—in the Greek, the word "assist" is translated paristēmi and it means "stand beside; be at hand; yield." So Paul told the Believers—men and women alike—to yield to a woman in the ministry, one who was an overseer.

Paul called Phoebe a "succoure," which is translated as prostatis in the Greek; this is defined as "a woman set over others." So Phoebe was a deacon and woman of great authority, who Paul was sending to the church to help them get established. Paul even credited Phoebe as being instrumental in getting his own ministry established. But Phoebe was just one of many women Paul acknowledged.

Other female leaders included Mary, Tryphene and Tryphosa, who Paul referred to as "laborers in the Lord" (Romans 16:6, 12); Andronicus and Junia, who Paul specifically called apostles (Romans 16:7); Aquila and Priscilla, who Paul referred to as co-laborers and pastors of a church in 1 Corinthians 16:19 (and most scholars believe Priscilla wasn't merely an assistant to her husband in leadership, but she carried equal authority). Paul also commended Euodia and Syntyche as co-laborers (Philippians 4:2).

Regarding those Paul called his co-laborers in the ministry, he said, "And we beseech you, brethren, to know them which labour among you, and are over you in the Lord, and admonish you" (1 Thessalonians 5:12). Each of these women were acknowledged as being "over" those in the church, operating as pastors and apostles, deacons and administrators. So nowhere in Scripture does Paul say women aren't allowed to preach, teach and lead.

Why then did Paul tell the women to be quiet in 1 Timothy 2:11-12? His instruction to the women to be silent was directed at that particular group of women, not all women. The problem with the women in this particular church (of Ephesus) was they were disrupting the service with their questions, and they were unlearned in the word of God. So Paul instructed them to save their questions for their husbands...at home. And since they were uneducated in the word of God, they weren't fit to lead in the church. It's also noted by scholars that the women in this church were attempting to gain respect in the church using their looks rather than by becoming Christ-like in character.

I would also like to add the fact that it was Paul who wrote, "There is neither Jew nor Gentile, neither slave nor free, nor is there male and female, for you are all one in Christ Jesus" (Galatians 3:28, NIV). He acknowledged that gender roles don't apply to the work of ministry, to the use of Kingdom authority. All people, male and female alike, have the power and authority—and might I add, the mandate of Christ found in the Great Commission—to make disciples of all nations by teaching and preaching the Gospel, cast out demons, lay hands on the sick, raise the dead, perform miracles, prophesy and more in Jesus' name. In fact, it was Jesus Himself who deputized both men and women to evangelize in His name. In Luke 8:1-3, several of His female disciples were listed. And in Luke chapter 10, the Bible says Jesus had at one point over seventy disciples, all of which He sent out to preach the Gospel from town to town—among that number were both male and female disciples.

*

I'll be honest and admit that it took me a while also to come to grips with the truth. I mean, God had given me the call, He spoke clearly into my spirit about my assignment, He backed up His utterance with His word, and then took me on a journey to show me in the Bible that the prohibition against women preachers was un-biblical; and yet, despite all of that, I still wrestled with accepting my calling and embracing the idea of being a women preacher. I understand just how deeply en-trenched tradition can be, and how it can literally cause us to argue with the word of God, which is the truth and final authority. Even when we know the truth, it takes a while sometimes for that truth to sink into our hearts. That's why we have to continually speak the word of God to ourselves—this is part of the process of renewing our minds so that we'll begin to think the right way and take on the right perspective.

The Bible says, "meditate" on God's word "night and day" (Joshua 1:8). Therefore, the more I read the Bi-ble and studied what it said about women in ministry, the more I began to accept the truth and shed the lies I'd been taught all my life. The more I studied God's word, the more I came face to face with the truth, and day after day, that truth chipped away at the religious indoc-trination I'd been groomed in. After a while, I became thoroughly convinced that I was called by God and that God had more in store for me than what I was seeing. I'd become completely convinced that the same power of God I read about in the Bible was the same power that was available to me, and that God wanted to use me to do the same things that Jesus did. I had to keep reading and repeating John 14:12 to myself until it finally sunk in that I was called to both preach and walk in the miracu-lous:

"I tell you the truth, anyone who believes in me will do the same works I have done, and even greater works, because I am going to be with the Father." (NLT)

Finally, I'd had it up to here with religion. I was tired of that bondage. I began to see what was behind that bondage: fear. God didn't give us a spirit of fear because fear brings torment and it causes us to operate with a controlling spirit (witchcraft) (2 Timothy 1:7; 1 John 4:18). John lists fear as the total opposite of God's love, which liberates us and allows us to liberate others (1 John 4:7-21).

Religion teaches us to live in fear, but God teaches us through His word to operate in love. When walking in love, we're not concerned with whether or not the vessel God is using is a male or female; we're concerned with whether or not the lost are hearing the Gospel and being saved. Souls become our priority, not power.

Jesus had to train His disciples out of that power-seeking attitude, that mentality of elitism and status. He told them, "Jesus said to them, 'The kings of the Gentiles lord it over them; and those who exercise authority over them call themselves Benefactors. But you are not to be like that. Instead, the greatest among you should be like the youngest, and the one who rules like the one who serves'" (Luke 22:25-26, NIV). Prior to that, the disciples were arguing with each other over who was the greatest among them. They were judging and comparing themselves to one another to see who deserved to be in power. They were simply concerned with their own egos, their own sense of power, and with exalting themselves. And yet, when we truly submit to Christ and take on His heart, selfish ambition and status will no longer be our goal, our number one concern. Those things won't even be on our radar.

It's crucial that we unlearn religion—that we unlearn the lies that have been drilled into our heads by people who didn't have the full understanding of Scripture. The only way to do this is to carefully and diligently study the word of God and be prepared to have your thinking and beliefs challenged by it. Don't try to make the word conform to your beliefs; let you beliefs conform to God's word. Do what James said and "receive with meekness the engrafted word, which is able to save your souls" (James 1:21). The word "meekness" there is translated prautēs in the Greek, and it means "mildness of disposition; gentleness of spirit; humility." When you come across a revelation in the Bible that conflicts with what you've been told or taught, don't fight the truth; instead, humbly accept the truth. Drop your pride and say, This is the truth, and I just need to accept it. Don't buck and fight against God. Don't let pride get in the way of your spiritual growth and your blessings. Quit arguing with God and humble yourself before His word, which should be the final authority in your life. Don't try to twist the scriptures around to accommodate you and what you're trying to do. If you've been doing this, repent. Say, "Lord, I'm sorry for fighting against you and attempting to twist your word for my personal and selfish gain. I humbly submit to your word today." And as you continue along this journey of unlearning lies, you'll have to repeat that prayer several more times. Your flesh is going to fight God every step of the way, but keep persisting. Keep moving forward. Keep repenting and speaking God's word out loud. Keep meditating on the word of God and allowing it to expose and change those erroneous, deeply held beliefs that the enemy has planted in your heart. Pretty soon, you'll be thoroughly convinced of the truth, too.

Chapter 2

LEAVING THE PEWS

I'D SILENTLY AND SECRETLY ACCEPTED THE CALL into ministry, but I was reluctant to announce it to others. Yes, I was thoroughly convinced that this is what God wanted me to do, but I wasn't willing to deal with the backlash that would come from the congregation. I thought about when Jesus stood before His hometown crowd in Nazareth and announced His calling, telling them He was the messiah that was prophesied to come. I imagined how they looked at Him. They thought He was crazy, and that He'd hit His head on a rock before entering the Synagogue. That's just before they attempted to throw Him over a cliff to His death.

I thought to myself, Hopefully, they won't haul me out of the sanctuary and try to throw me over a cliff. News headline would read: "Poor, delusional woman thought she was called to be a preacher, and she was tossed into the ocean by the members of her congregation at the behest of the pastor. She was survived by her ex-husband and daughter."

I decided to keep that information to myself; I didn't want that heat coming down on my head. Instead, I took another route and decided that I could still fulfill my calling in other ways.

By this time, I had gotten a divorce from my husband and moved to another state. While there, I joined another ministry. It was a Baptist Church like the one I'd left, so I felt at home there. I began working with different ministries within the church: Sunday School, Children's Ministry, the Mission Board, and other auxiliaries. I began serving wherever I could, stealing small opportunities display my gift for teaching and ministering. I especially loved doing the Sunday morning announcements during service. Of course, I had to add my brand of fire, my little flare and get the audience pumped up.

I was quickly developing a reputation in the church. People knew me as a good teacher of the Word, as an individual on fire for God. They called on me often to do the announcements and set the atmosphere in the congregation. I was doing everything but the thing God called me to do. And sadly, I was trying to force myself to be okay with this.

But when God calls you to preach, He doesn't mean preach from the pews.

*

I grappled with the call of ministry mainly because I knew what it meant. Being an ordained minister is a great responsibility; it means you're more than a member who's relegated to the pews; instead, you're a leader who stands out. Everyone looks to you for leadership and guidance when you're a minister. They expect more from you than everyone else. You become a shining light on a hill, the only representation of God some people see.

I didn't want to stand out. I preferred to blend in with the crowd. But God was calling me out of the crowd. He was making me a leader. That meant I'd have to take the hits and the criticism, but it also meant I'd get to establish a new precedent and break barriers in the church. This was my chance to change things for the better, to get rid of the hindrances I discovered holding God's people back.

It's funny how we always ask God to change people and situations but hesitate when God chooses to do so through us. We usually prefer that God do these things through someone else. But be prepared to be called out by God. Be prepared to hear Him say, Sure, I'll break barriers and demolish strongholds in others, but I'm going to use you to do it. I'm going to send you to accomplish this task.

Here's the sad truth: Most people are afraid of being used by God. They are afraid of being His vessel. They want to remain in their comfort zones. And I get it. It's scary leaving the comfort zone and stepping onto the battlefield. It feels good maintaining an ordered existence where nothing happens out of the ordinary and you can maintain a sense of control. On the other hand, following God can be scary. God may lead you into a wilderness like He did Jesus and bring you face to face with devils you never knew existed. God might take you to far away lands you never imagined being. You could end up in Africa, serving in an underprivileged village that's surrounded by lions and hyenas, facing diseases you never heard of. You could end up in the North Pole preaching to the Eskimos while surrounded by polar bears. You never know what to expect with God.

And not only does God have a tendency to send us places that are foreign to us, but He instructs us to do things we've never done before. He'll put us in intimidating environments and then tell us to do the strangest things. How would you feel standing before a 10 foot tall giant with a slingshot? Or marching seven times around the unscalable walls of a mighty city? Or fighting an army of over three-hundred thousand Midianites with only six-hundred men? Or standing before the most powerful man in the world (Pharaoh) commanding the most powerful army on the planet with nothing but a stick? Crazy! I know. And yet, God often instructs us to do crazy things, things that don't make sense to us; that's frustrating and scary enough by itself. But it's a part of the call.

God isn't looking for wimps. He's not looking for people who'll back away from a challenge, people with thin skin. I hate to admit it, but the ministry requires thick skin. You have to be tough. Think about it. When God called Jeremiah into the ministry, what was Jeremiah's response? He said,

CHAPTER 2: LEAVING THE PEWS

"'Alas, Sovereign LORD,'" I said, "I do not know how to speak; I am too young.'

However, God's response to Him was,

"'Do not say, 'I am too young.' You must go to everyone I send you to and say whatever I command you. Do not be afraid of them, for I am with you and will rescue you...'Get yourself ready! Stand up and say to them whatever I command you. Do not be terrified by them, or I will terrify you before them. Today I have made you a fortified city, an iron pillar and a bronze wall to stand against the whole land—against the kings of Judah, its officials, its priests and the people of the land. They will fight against you but will not overcome you, for I am with you and will rescue you,' declares the LORD." (Jeremiah 1:7-8, 17-19, NIV)

In other words, God told Jeremiah to toughen up. He informed Jeremiah that he needed to be prepared for challenges, for opposition and obstacles. He let Jeremiah know that everyone wasn't going to accept him and the call on his life, but he couldn't allow that to deter him. God even told Jeremiah He was making him a "fortified city, an iron pillar and bronze wall." That meant He was making Jeremiah tough, rough, hard. So when men looked at him like he was unqualified and unworthy to deliver the word of the Lord to them, he'd look them in the eyes with confidence rather than cower in fear and say what God told him to say. In other words, God was making Jeremiah a lion, someone who wouldn't be afraid of anyone, a soldier.

Are you a soldier? If you're a child of God, that's what God calls you. He calls you a soldier in the army of the Lord. Paul wrote in 2 Timothy 2:3-4, "Join with me in suffering, like a good soldier of Christ Jesus. No one serving as a soldier gets entangled in civilian affairs, but rather tries to please his commanding officer" (NIV). Your commanding officer is God; your mission is souls. You've been planted on this earth, behind enemy lines, but you've been given superior weapons to defeat the enemy. Paul revealed this in Ephesians 6:13-17,

> "Therefore put on the full armor of God, so that when the day of evil comes, you may be able to stand your ground, and after you have done everything, to stand. Stand firm then, with the belt of truth buckled around your waist, with the breastplate of righteousness in place, and with your feet fitted with the readiness that comes from the gospel of peace. In addition to all this, take up the shield of faith, with which you can extinguish all the flaming arrows of the evil one. Take the helmet of salvation and the sword of the Spirit, which is the word of God." (NIV)

And also in 2 Corinthians 10:4-5, he wrote,

CHAPTER 2: LEAVING THE PEWS

"The weapons we fight with are not the weapons of the world. On the contrary, they have divine power to demolish strongholds. We demolish arguments and every pretension that sets itself up against the knowledge of God, and we take captive every thought to make it obedient to Christ." (NIV)

Be brave. Be tough. Be bold and fear no man. God doesn't want us to live in fear. He didn't give us a "spirit of fear" according to 2 Timothy 1:7. The word "fear" is translated deilia in the Greek, and it means "timidity; cowardice." In other words, God didn't make us cowards; He didn't design us to be timid ("showing a lack of courage or confidence; easily frightened"). He designed us instead to be bold, courageous and fearless. God endowed us with power over demons. In Satan's eyes, we are bogeymen. We scare the Hell out of Hell's forces. When we walk through the door, demons know our names and whose authority we operate in and run for the hills.

Do you know who you are as a child of God? Do you really know? If you knew, you'd be excited over the challenge rather than fearful.

I'll admit I was timid, afraid, nervous of what the members of the church and the pastor would say had I announced to them my calling. But God has a way of pushing us into our destinies. You see, it's one thing when God calls you, and another when you call yourself. When God calls you, He'll arrange the circumstances and cause doors to open for you. But when you call yourself, you'll try to make things happen only to fail.

A DIVINE SHOVE

God shoved me into the ministry using people. He began to confirm to me my calling through the people around me.

Here's a word of wisdom: The Bible says in Proverbs 27:2,

> "Let someone else praise you, and not your own mouth; an outsider, and not your own lips." (NIV)

Solomon also wrote,

> "Do not exalt yourself in the king's presence, and do not claim a place among his great men; it is better for him to say to you, "Come up here," than for him to humiliate you before his nobles..." (Proverbs 25:6-7, NIV)

Some of you who're reading this book who may feel like you're called by God to the ministry, and you may be tempted to run out and print up a bunch of business cards with your name and the self-imposed title "Minister, Reverend, Evangelist, Prophet, Pastor" on them. But take my advice and avoid that mistake. Let God confirm your calling rather than trying to force others to recognize your alleged calling. If God calls you into the ministry, He will also confirm you before men.

Ah! I just touched on a revelation, a biblical

principle each of us should understand. That revelation is that God does the calling and the confirming. That principle is found in Matthew 3:13-17. There we read,

> "Then Jesus came from Galilee to the Jordan to be baptized by John. But John tried to deter him, saying, 'I need to be baptized by you, and do you come to me?' Jesus replied, 'Let it be so now; it is proper for us to do this to fulfill all righteousness.' Then John consented. As soon as Jesus was baptized, he went up out of the water. At that moment heaven was opened, and he saw the Spirit of God descending like a dove and alighting on him. And a voice from heaven said, 'This is my Son, whom I love; with him I am well pleased.'" (NIV)

Notice a few things here: Jesus was more anointed than John the Baptist, but He had to humble Himself before John in order to be endorsed by the Father. Jesus had to practice humility before He could be exalted. That's what Peter told us we must do, "In the same way, you younger men must accept the authority of the elders. And all of you, serve each other in humility, for God opposes the proud but favors the humble. So humble yourselves under the mighty power of God, and at the right time he will lift you up in honor" (1 Peter 5:5-6, NLT). Even Jesus wasn't exempt from this rule. It doesn't matter how gifted you are, how anointed you are, how long you've been in church, and what Bible college or university you graduated from; God will not exalt you if you're in the business of exalting yourself. You have to humble yourself before those God has placed over you. When you do this, God will bring elevation into your life.

After Jesus humbled Himself before John the Baptist and received His baptism, that's when the Heavenly Father uttered the words from the Heavens, "This is my Son, whom I love; with him I am well pleased." That was the confirmation Jesus needed to begin His earthly ministry.

But wait! Not so fast! Jesus didn't just launch out into ministry right then. After the Father announced Him before men, the Holy Spirit sent Him into the desert to be tested by the devil. Why is this so important? It's because you're not ready to step into the ministry if you haven't been tried and tested. If you're not ready for the attacks of the enemy, you're not ready to stand in anyone's pulpit. If you're not ready to face problems, persecution, deal with pressure, endure criticism and overcome the temptations of the flesh, don't step foot into a pulpit. God has to test you first. God has to afflict you with adversity and trials that reveal what's really inside you. Some of us think we're ready, but we're not. We see the ministry and get wowed by all of the pageantry, thinking it's going to be a cake walk. We think all we have to do is stand behind a podium and deliver a carefully crafted sermon like we're delivering a speech in a classroom. But it's a lot more than that. You have souls in your hand, and if you're not ready for that responsibility, you'll deal significant damage to God's Kingdom

(Hebrews 6:4-6; Hebrews 12:15).

James 3:1 says, "Dear brothers and sisters, not many of you should become teachers in the church, for we who teach will be judged more strictly" (NLT). That means those who are ministers are held to a higher level of accountability in God's eyes. They must be careful not to mislead God's people by saying the wrong things and setting the wrong example. The ministry is tough, and it requires spiritually mature, battle-tested, doctrinally sound people. So don't be in a rush to jump into the pulpit. Take your time. God knows when you're ready. Like He said in our earlier scripture, "At the right time he will lift you up in honor."

Although David was called to lead, he didn't become king right away. It took over a decade for David to lead. God tested him in the wilderness. I believe the biggest test David underwent was found in 1 Samuel chapter 26. There, King Saul, who was hunting David and his men, went to rest in a cave, not knowing David and his men were hiding in that same cave. While Saul slept, David and one of his men, Abner, hovered over Saul's body. David had the opportunity to kill the man that had caused him so much pain. King Saul did David wrong. He committed so much evil against David. And not only that, but King Saul was the only obstacle between David and the throne. So it would have seemed fitting that David and his men killed Saul. And yet, David warned his men,

"But David said to Abishai, 'Don't destroy him!

Who can lay a hand on the LORD's anointed and be guiltless? As surely as the LORD lives,' he said, 'the LORD himself will strike him, or his time will come and he will die, or he will go into battle and perish. But the LORD forbid that I should lay a hand on the LORD's anointed. Now get the spear and water jug that are near his head, and let's go.'" (NIV)

That was a test of honor. Although King Saul mistreated David, God still expected David to honor him. You know you're battle-tested when you can compose yourself in the face of great opposition, smile when people are insulting, bless people who're attacking you and trying to destroy you, help people who hurt you, serve people who mistreat you, do good to people who do you wrong, and honor people in authority who behave dishonorable. When you can put yourself on the back-burner and show honor and respect to the leaders appointed by God to "keep watch over you as those who must give an account" (Hebrews 13:17, NIV), then you're ready for elevation.

God called me into the ministry, but I didn't jump up and promote myself. I didn't get in the pastor's face and demand that he accept my calling. I simply served where I could, giving it my all in everything I did around the church. People began to notice my gift and approach me. God sent the confirmation my way.

I remember a sweet old lady who used to come up to me every Sunday and say, "Lea, you missed your calling." She never missed a beat. Week after week, she reminded me that I was called by God to do more than the announcements and teach Sunday School. God kept reminding me of His calling through different individuals.

One day, I shared the news of my calling with a close friend of mine. I didn't know what her response would be. I figured she'd think I was crazy and laugh at me, or maybe even scold me. But I was shocked by her response. "Leander, I don't doubt it for a minute. Go for it," she responded. I told her I didn't feel qualified or capable, but she replied, "Lea, I heard you. You're supposed to be in ministry." To her, it was obvious that I was called to the ministry. She was waiting for me to come to terms with God's will for me.

But, believe it or not, the biggest confirmation came from my pastor. One Saturday morning, I was responsible for overseeing the prayer service at church. That weekend, my family was coming to town to fellowship with me at church. During this time, the nudge of the Holy Spirit in my heart to share with my pastor the calling on my life grew stronger. He kept pushing me to tell the pastor, so I did. I went to the pastor that Saturday and said, "Pastor, I feel like God has called me into the ministry." His response took me aback. He responded,

"Leander, I don't doubt that for one minute." Whoah! I thought. I was shocked. I'd been sitting and serving in his ministry for the past seven years and never knew he recognized the call of God on my life because

49

he never said anything to me. He just watched my faithfulness in serving over the years.

"But pastor, I don't feel capable or qualified," I retorted.

"If you did, I would have a problem with it," he replied. "Isn't your family coming this weekend?"

"Yes."

"Good! I want you to announce to the congregation your calling this Sunday then."

I couldn't believe it. I was speechless. My heart was leaping within me when he said that.

That Sunday, during service, I got up and announced before the church that God called me to preach. Many within the audience erupted in celebration. That nice old lady that constantly reminded me of my calling was jumping up and down and shouting, "I knew it! I knew it!" You'd think she was my mother the way she was acting. Everyone who knew me was overjoyed and filled with excitement. A seven-year journey had come to an end and I was finally being recognized as a minister of the Gospel by an authentic pastor. That was the year 1994, the year I gave my trial sermon and received my license in the ministry.

The following year, I moved to Georgia and joined Mount Carmel Baptist Church under the leadership of Reverend Timothy Flemming, Sr. Again, I didn't try to promote myself. I didn't advertise my calling to anyone. I didn't ask the pastor to put me on the ministry staff. Instead, God moved over the pastor to call me out and acknowledge my calling.

CHAPTER 2: LEAVING THE PEWS

One Sunday morning, during service, Pastor Flemming looked at me and said, "Leander, God said it's time for you to leave the Mother's Board and take your rightful place in the ministry." He confirmed again that I didn't belong in the back, that I wasn't called by God to blend in with the crowd; instead, I belonged in the forefront as a minister, a leader. I left the Mother's Board and moved into position where I belonged. And that year, I received my ordination as a minister of the Gospel.

*

I discovered the importance of allowing God to orchestrate the circumstances of my life rather than trying to do things on my own. Like the Bible says, "Moreover whom he did predestinate, them he also called: and whom he called, them he also justified: and whom he justified, them he also glorified" (Romans 8:30). God is a master at qualifying those He calls. He'll do the work of elevating you.

When God calls you, He'll make sure you get to where you belong. Nothing will be able to stop the call of God on your life...when it's your turn to walk in it. And that's the key: when it's your turn. God knows when you're ready. After you've been tried and have proven yourself ready for the responsibility of the ministry, God will move mountains to usher you into your destiny. He'll send people to speak into your life and confirm your calling. But you must allow God to do it.

Furthermore, it's important that you realize the

ministry is only the beginning. There is much more God wants to do in and through you. God not only desires to use your mouth as His mouthpiece, but He desires to demonstrate His power and goodness through your life. But in order for that to happen, He'll need to break some chains off of you like He had to do in my life. For what good is it to set others free while you're still bound. And I was certainly bound, but didn't know it.

Chapter 3

A WOUNDED SOUL

I LOVE HEARING THE STORY ABOUT THE THREE Hebrew boys, Shadrach, Meshach and Abednego from Daniel, the third chapter. They refused to bow the knee before a false god and were punished for it. King Nebuchadnezzar ordered his guards to place them in a fiery furnace. God got in the furnace with them and shielded them from the flames, and they were able to come out of the fire and not smell like smoke.

God can protect people in the midst of their fiery furnaces and erase any evidence they were even in the flames. But that wasn't the case with me. You could smell the smoke in my clothes. Smoke was still rising from my hair. My skin was still smoldering. Heck, the fire burned my eyebrows off!

I didn't go through years of religious abuse unscathed. I wish I could say otherwise, but I can't. I felt hurt. I had sustained scars on my soul. But I didn't know how badly scarred I was. I didn't know how deep the wounds on my soul went.

We all get wounded. No one goes through life unscathed. So it's okay to not be okay. But it's not okay to let your wounds fester and turn into bitterness like mine did. The scary thing is I didn't know I'd become bitter as a result of the religious abuse I experienced, but thankfully, God knew, and He was about to bring it to my attention.

*

In 2008, I moved back to Louisiana to take care of my mother who'd fallen ill. By this time, I'd traveled a little bit and received my license and ordination as a minister. I'd preached in many pulpits and had gotten used to walking in my calling as a minister of the Gospel. But, now, I was back home and had started attending my mom's church. I even joined the church. But when I went to the pastor and informed him that I was an ordained minster, he looked at me funnily and told me he wasn't having it—he refused to allow a woman to preach in his pulpit. And every so often, he'd get up in the pulpit and remind everyone (basically, he was talking to me) "a woman will never preach in this pulpit."

I found myself dealing with the same religious bondage I escaped years prior. And even though I humbled myself and tried to serve faithfully, there was a nagging pain in my heart. I felt so restricted, so bound. I felt like I was under a heavy weight of oppression, and I was. Again, I was back under religious bondage.

Now, I have to be honest and admit that I can't

say it was God who told me to join that church. Many times, we do things on our own without consulting the Holy Spirit, and find ourselves in precarious situations as a result thereof. I was in a place that was draining the life out of me. There I was, serving on the New Members Orientation staff, teaching the new members, but I felt like the walking dead. The joy was being sucked out of me week after week. Slowly, I began to disregard my own calling. Because the pastor didn't accept and acknowledge women preachers, I stopped acknowledging my title. Whenever guess ministers came and asked for all ministers to stand, I remained seated. I felt the confidence I once had beginning to leave. Little by little, the religious abuse was starting to wear me down. It was eating away at my soul gradually.

There are some environments you can't remain in once God places His hand on you. I thought I had to submit under that pastor and remain there because it pleased God. Also, I told myself that wherever I went, I was going to encounter problems, so why not endure this one. But, looking back, I realize that was a mistake. I had a choice in the matter. I didn't have to subject myself to that kind of treatment and remain in that church. I didn't have to sit Sunday after Sunday and listen to a misguided leader subtly berate me from the pulpit until my self-esteem was torn down.

The Apostle Paul warns us against remaining in the wrong atmospheres. He said in 1 Corinthians 15:33, "Do not be misled: 'Bad company corrupts good character'" (NIV). In my case, the bad company I kept was a religious crowd who fought against the Word of God. I'd planted myself in a ministry that didn't want to embrace God's truth and break manmade, demonic traditions. Rather worldly or religious bondage, bondage is still bondage. But to be honest, religious bondage is probably worse. Most secular sinners know they are living in sin, but religious sinners often believe they are serving God while doing the devil's work. That's what Jesus had to deal with in John 8:31-45 where He explained to the Jews who were fighting Him, "If God were your Father, you would love me, for I have come here from God. I have not come on my own; God sent me. Why is my language not clear to you? Because you are unable to hear what I say. You belong to your father, the devil, and you want to carry out your father's desires" (vs. 42-45). Those Jews truly believed they were serving God, so imagine the shock on their faces when Jesus informed them they were really serving Satan because of their unwillingness to submit to the truth. They were too religious for Christ. They preferred tradition over truth. And for that reason, Jesus left them alone.

Stop trying to change people who don't want to change. Their burdens are not your responsibility. If they want God, they know how to call on Him. If they want deliverance, they know how to turn to God. If they're broke, they know how to ask God for a financial blessing. Sometimes, you have to let people go through on their own so they'll wake up and stop "playing church." But realize that you don't have to join yourself to someone who's unequally yoked," and that includes people in the church who're hostile to the move of God in your life.

Again, I'm not telling you to become a rogue Christian and do things on your own. I certainly don't agree with the idea of running from church to church to get what you want—if that pastor doesn't acknowledge you or give in to your demands, you then leave and look another church. That's witchcraft! 1 Samuel 15:23 says, "For rebellion is as the sin of witchcraft." Witchcraft is where you try to control people, including God, in an attempt to get what you want. You're not submitted to God, and you're not submitted to another like Peter instructed us. You're only concerned about yourself.

However, it's another thing to deliberately place yourself in an abusive environment. You must be led by God to the right church. When you're anointed, you must stay in an atmosphere that respects the anointing. Get around people who will stir up your faith while holding you accountable to the Gospel.

I didn't belong in that church. I was only there because of my mom. But that wasn't a place for me to grow. Like a victim of domestic violence, I stayed where I didn't need to be longer than I intended to stay. I stayed there for five years and started getting comfortable there. Not even David remained in King Saul's presence after Saul went crazy. David honored Saul, but he had enough sense to get away from Saul. He didn't stand there and let Saul pin him to the wall with a spear or cut his head off. You can love people from a distance. You can forgive and be kind to people without compromising your standards and allowing them to cross your boundaries.

Ultimately, I was doing damage to myself by staying there. I didn't realize how bitter I'd become until one day, I enrolled in a program to become a licensed counselor. While in the program, I was having a conversation with one of my classmates when my pastor's name came up. When his name was mentioned, I felt anger, resentment and animosity rise inside me and I realized I was secretly bitter toward him. I mean, I felt like exploding with anger. I had to go to God and ask Him to heal my heart and deal with my inner wounds.

ROOTS

Now, I could have become one of those angry women who preach out of bitterness. I see and hear plenty of them. Rather than talking about Christ, they spend half of their time talking about how unfair many churches are. They try to connect with other women through pain, and get them to side with them against what they think is a male dominated culture. These are religious feminists. They sneer at men as if they hate them. They do the same thing the men trapped in deception do: discriminate against people based on gender.

You can't defeat the devil by acting like the devil. I knew that. And that's why I chose a different route. I didn't want to leave the church bitterly. I didn't want to serve there while bitter either. I wanted to clear my heart so I could remain in right standing with God. Jesus explained to us that we must forgive others if we want God to forgive us. Furthermore, the author of Hebrews warned us against allowing a "root of bitterness" to spring up within and defile others (Hebrews 12:15).

Before the blade pops up and the tree and its branches form, roots spread beneath the surface; the deeper the roots, the stronger the tree. Roots are unseen. They're hidden. It's not until later that you discover a seed had been planted. When bitter, resentment and anger secretly form in your heart. You know, Satan would like nothing more than to let you climb the mountain of success only to expose and humiliate you on the big stage. God doesn't want you to reach the mountaintop while harboring anger and bitterness. He wants to heal you before you ascend the mountain. That's why some of us are not seeing the elevation we desire from God. Our hearts aren't right. Our motives aren't pure. We want to "make it" so that we can prove to our haters that we've arrived. We simply want to prove something to certain people in our lives.

James 4:2-3 says, "You want what you don't have, so you scheme and kill to get it. You are jealous of what others have, but you can't get it, so you fight and wage war to take it away from them. Yet you don't have what you want because you don't ask God for it. And even when you ask, you don't get it because your motives are all wrong—you want only what will give you pleasure" (NLT). When bitter and angry, your motivation for serving will always be wrong. You'll be focused on revenge and proving yourself to someone. God wants us to serve Him and others out of love, with hearts of gladness. Don't seek to preach because you want a title. Don't look at the ministry and think that receiving special recognition will fill the emptiness in your heart and give you the validation in life you crave. These are the wrong motives to have. So let God free you from the emotional bondages you may be facing first, and then you'll be ready to handle the responsibility of ministry.

To deal with the issues of the heart, we must first ask the Holy Spirit to reveal to us any hidden roots of bitterness inside us. He knows what's in our hearts more than anyone one else, including us. The Bible says,

> "The human heart is the most deceitful of all things, and desperately wicked. Who really knows how bad it is? But I, the LORD, search all hearts and examine secret motives. I give all people their due rewards, according to what their actions deserve." (Jeremiah 17:9-10, NLT)

Leave it up to the Holy Spirit to reveal to you what's really inside of you.

After God reveals to you the hidden things in your heart, forgive those who hurt you. This is important because, without forgiveness, your faith won't work and God can't forgive you of your sins according to Mark 11:23-26. Many ministers want God to speak to them and use them mightily in the pulpit, but they're unwilling to forgive the people who hurt them, and their unforgiving attitudes are hindering them from hearing from God and experiencing His power. We must forgive.

CHAPTER 3: A WOUNDED SOUL

When God brought it to my attention that I was secretly bitter against my pastor, I realized I needed to get that bitterness out of my heart. If I allowed bitterness to remain in my heart, I would have missed every blessing God had for me. So I contacted the pastor's assistant to schedule a meeting with the pastor. That Wednesday, we met. That's when I told him,

"Pastor, I owe you an apology."

Confused, he responded, "An apology?"

"Yes, because I feel I have some anger and animosity; the Lord has brought this to my attention. I know I'm called of God but you won't acknowledge me as a minister, and I can't go forward because I 'm under your leadership. And being that I'm under someone else's leadership, there can't be two heads; you have to be able to follow. And since the lord has planted me here, I can't go over and above what you allow me to do."

"Sister, that's big!" he commented. "Well, do you know my position on women ministers?"

"All I know is what you told me—that you don't believe in women ministers."

"No, I don't believe a woman can teach a man. Do you realize that when you're in a congregation and you stand up, a man isn't going to hear what you say because he's going to be looking at you as an individual."

"Well, brother, he needs some deliverance. That's his problem, not mine. If the Word is going forward, that's what the focus needs to be on, not who I am or what I look like."

Afterwards, the pastor and his assistant mentioned Prophetess Juanita Bynum. It dawned on me that the conversation wasn't going anywhere, but I was content that I'd done what was necessary to clear my heart.

It didn't matter if the pastor agreed with me or not. What mattered is that I released the bitterness from my heart and allowed God to heal it. Healing doesn't come from people. I realized I didn't need the pastor to validate and affirm me; God did it. I simply needed to remove the blockage standing in the way of the move of God in my life. And that's what I did. I forgave, and afterwards, saw the hand of God move in my life like never before.

Forgive. Don't worry about what happens to the person you forgive; God will deal with them. But do your job and let go of the hurt inflicted on you by others. Let it go so you can receive what God has for you.

Forgiveness and walking in humility is the key to receiving the blessings and favor of God in your life. And as you'll discover in the next chapter, God has more in store for you than you know. He anxiously desires to release blessings in your life, but you have to pass the test of forgiveness first.

Chapter 4

SUPERNATURAL PROVISIONS

REMEMBER WHEN I SAID GOD WANTS TO preach through our lives and not just our mouths? Well, I am a living testimony of that. God wants to use our lives as His sermon. People will listen to your words, but ignore them if they don't see the fruit of God's favor in your life. That's one of the problems with many Christians today: they talk about a God who is rich in houses and land, but they can't afford to pay their rent. Many Christians brag about a God who is a healer, but they stay sick. They talk about having the victory in their lives, but they live defeated lives. Churches try to lure people in with promises of a blessed life, but when people step through their doors and see nothing but broke and struggling people, they turn and walk away. How can we talk about the goodness of God to when we can't experience it for ourselves?

WHO SAID A WOMAN CAN'T PREACH?

The Bible says,

> "So even though wisdom is better than strength, those who are wise will be despised if they are poor. What they say will not be appreciated for long." (Ecclesiastes 9:16, NLT)

That's where many within the church are. They have wisdom, but the world doesn't want to receive from them because they lack substance; there's no evidence their wisdom works. People watch your life more than they listen to your words.

Here's the reality: every Believer has the favor of God on them, but not every Believer knows how to walk in it. Many people are practicing religion rather than Christianity, and there's a difference between the two. Religion is manmade. Christianity is not a religion; it is a lifestyle that entails being led by the Holy Spirit into the perfect will of God for one's life. In short, religion is being led by man, while Christianity is being led by God. And where does God want to lead us?

That's a good question.

God desires to lead us into the blessings He has prepared for us before we were even born. Yes, God designed your life before you got here. He designed every detail of it. There's not one thing He overlooked or missed. God knows who you are and where you're supposed to be, what you're supposed to be doing in life, and everything about your personality, from your quirks and pet-peeves to your passions and dreams. As the Apostle Paul put it,

> "For we are God's masterpiece. He has created
> us anew in Christ Jesus, so we can do the good
> things he planned for us long ago." (Ephesians
> 2:10, NLT)

Stop judging yourself because of other people's opinions
of you. God made you just the way He wanted to. You're
exactly who you're supposed to be. Satan loves to attack
our self-esteem by attacking our sense of identity, especially with all of the identity-confusion taking place in
our culture today. Satan wants you to think you were
born in the wrong body, with the wrong skin color, the
wrong hair, into the wrong family, on the wrong side
of the tracks, under the wrong circumstances, with the
wrong personality, and more. He wants you to wallow
in confusion over who you are. He endeavors to keep us
blind to the truth about who they are. And he accom-
plishes this, first and foremost, by causing us to avoid
seeking God, our Creator and the only one who knows
our purpose for existing. We turn to people for a sense
of purpose and identity, sit at the feet of gurus and sag-
es, immerse ourselves in books and everything we can
get our hands on that promises us spiritual enlighten-
ment; and yet, only Christ can reveal to us our identities
and purposes.

Only through hearing the voice of the Savior can
we discover our paths in life. Now, I know what I'm saying isn't politically correct. Heck, what I'm saying isn't

even religiously endorsed. Many within the "religious" community reject the notion that the Holy Spirit is a real person who seeks to lead and guide us. Many people view God as some far away observer who's emotionally unavailable, as one too busy to entertain our "petty" issues.

But can I share with you a revelation that will change your outlook if this is yours? Jesus said, "And the very hairs on your head are all numbered. So don't be afraid; you are more valuable to God than a whole flock of sparrows" (Luke 12:7, NLT). And David recorded in Psalm 56:8, "You keep track of all my sorrows. You have collected all my tears in your bottle. You have recorded each one in your book" (NLT). Does that sound like a God who's too busy to care about your concerns? Of course not. He cares. He sees. He knows. And He has a plan for you and I. But the secret to experiencing God's blessings is learning to hear His voice. I will dive into how to do that in the next chapter.

TIME TO MOVE

I'd heard God clearly. His instruction to me was unmistakable, even if hard to accept. And I must admit that when God speaks to us, His instructions won't always make sense. Perhaps, that's the most difficult part of this whole process. It's not that we don't hear God; it's simply that God's instructions don't make sense to us. We can't understand what God is telling us to do. We're trying to figure God out rather than trust Him.

It was 2006, and I was living in California when

CHAPTER 4: SUPERNATURAL PROVISIONS

I heard God tell me to pack up and leave. I was housing foster kids at the time. That was a challenge. Some kids would run away, some would really work to push my patience. But all in all, I loved what I was doing. Most of the kids were great. But God said my season there was up. He told me to contact Children's Services and tell them to pick up the kids, store my belongings in storage, and get a room. I didn't understand what God was doing at the time; it made no sense to me. But I believe it was because of my willingness to obey God's first instruction that He opened the door for me to experience the next blessing along the way. I had to say yes first and then take the first step before He unveiled the next part of His overall plan for me.

After calling Children's Services and taking the first step, I didn't know where I was going to move. But God had a plan. Suddenly, a friend of mine called me to congratulate me on my ordination as a minister. She then asked me, "How are the kids?"

"I just called Children's Services," I told her.

"Well, if you need a room, I have one." That was unexpected, but right on time. She offered the room to me free of charge. But I was not prepared for what God was about to do next.

One day, I received a call from a lady in California. She asked me, "Are you working?"

"No, I'm not at the moment."

"Well, will you consider working for me? You come highly recommended."

I thought about it for a moment. I wasn't interested in moving back to California at the moment, but then the lady made an offer it was hard to dismiss. She said, "I will pay you $7,000 a month to take care of my mother."

"Ma'am, I can't take that kind of money. I work ministry, plus I receive social security. So I'm not even able to take that kind of money."

"Well, we'll work it out," she replied. So I took the job. I moved in with her and she started out paying me $5000 cash every two weeks. I felt funny receiving so much money. I'd never received that much money before in my life. After a three months, I went to her and told her I needed to render to Caesar what is Caesar's—in other words, I needed to pay taxes off the income I was making to be fair. Her accountant set things up for me. Then she said to me, "Lee, this is what we can this. You've been here for three months. So we can give you up to $15,000, and let that be a gift. And we'll start your salary as of October."

I was blown away. But she continued and said, "What we'll do is, each year, we'll give you that $15,000 upfront. How do you want to do it? Pay you in one lump sum? Just let us know how you want us to pay you."

Again, my mind was blown. It seemed like one of those "too good to be true" things, but it was real. There was no catch. I worked there for nine months until that lady's mother passed. After that, I was expecting to be sent away, but the lady approached me and said, "You know you don't have to go anywhere, right? You can continue to stay with us. I'll even give you a raise, pay you more money if you stay." I couldn't believe what I was hearing. That caught me off guard.

I continued to housesit for that lady in California for several months. And suddenly, she decided to move from California to South Carolina. She wanted to sell her California estate. She'd purchased a beautiful home in Hilton Head and asked me to move in with her. And she offered me another raise. Suddenly, I found myself living in a brand new house with all expenses paid and having an even larger salary than before. That was nobody but God.

While making the transition to South Carolina, I stopped in Atlanta to visit a few people. I remember speaking with a friend of mine, Zadie. We'd met at Mt. Carmel Baptist Church. She asked me how everything was going, and I told her what God did. She then said to me, "Didn't the Lord tell us in His Word, He would give us houses we didn't build?" Those words began to resonate with me. It dawned on me I was living out Deuteronomy 6:11 where God made that promise to His people. The crazy thing is I didn't have to look for money. I didn't have to look for a job, a room, a house or anything else. God just gave me all of these things and more.

This is a picture of the divine provisions of God. He gives us sweat-less victories and causes us to prosper without effort. I know that's hard to understand and accept for many of us, but it's true. It's difficult to accept this as a reality when you've been bred your entire life to work hard for these things. You've been told since a child that you have to "make" things happen for you in life. We've been told that the only way to survive and thrive is to hustle hard, and even cut throats if necessary. We've even been made to believe that God's provisions are based on our "works". And yet, the Bible tells us, "For he that is entered into his rest, he also hath ceased from his own works, as God did from his" (Hebrews 4:10). That means we no longer have to toil and struggle to receive God's provisions and blessings, we no longer have to figure out what to do next or where our next meal is coming from. God wants us to rest from our cares and trust all of these things into His hands. The more we relax and trust Him, the more we'll see the manifestation of His goodness.

*

The provisions kept on coming. But I'll be honest and admit I didn't like how they were coming. I was glad God blessed me blessed me to live in a beautiful house, but I wanted my own house. I was grateful for His provisions, but I wanted to have something I could claim as my own. Sure, I was making a truck load of money, but there was still that nagging issue. I couldn't fully appreciate all God had done because He didn't do them my way.

I'm sure you probably struggle with this. Most people do. We want God to bless and provide for us, but we want Him to do it our way. We pray and ask God to meet our needs, but we complain about the way He meets them. God has a tendency of derailing our plans and putting us on detours we never expected. You ask

CHAPTER 4: SUPERNATURAL PROVISIONS

Him to bless you financially, but then you lose your job and find yourself in a legal battle. You ask God to bless your marriage, but then your child gets sick.

Look at the life of Joseph. God promised to bless Joseph mightily. God gave Joseph a dream one night where He revealed to Joseph that multitudes of people, including his father and siblings, would one day bow to him. But then, Joseph's life seemed to go haywire. His jealous brothers first threw him into a pit with intentions of murdering him, but they chose instead to sell him to a group of Egyptian merchants as a slave. And now, Joseph was a slave, wallowing away in chains in Potiphar's house. But just when you thought things couldn't get any worse, Mrs. Potiphar develops the hots for Joseph and tries to seduce him while her husband was away on business one day. Joseph did the right thing and ran, but not before she grabbed his garment and then yelled rape. Suddenly, Joseph went from bad to worse. He was now a prisoner in Pharaoh's dingy dungeon, left there to rot away. I'm pretty sure that's not what Joseph had in mind when God told him He was going to elevate him. Joseph never imagined the Hell, the pain, the suffering he'd endure on the way to the promise. However, it was Joseph's encounter with a specific person in that prison cell that opened the door for him to become the Prime Minister of Egypt. Had Joseph never gone through what he went through, he would have never been in the right place to meet the right person who could connect him to his destiny. In that prison cell, Joseph interpreted the dreams of two men: a baker and a cupbearer. That cupbearer was Pharaoh's personal servant. And when Pharaoh had a dream he couldn't understand on night, it was the cupbearer who told him about Joseph. After that, Joseph found himself standing before the most powerful man in the world, Pharaoh. And from there, the rest is history.

So, understand that God will bless you, but He most likely won't do it the way you want Him to or the way you're expecting Him to. He truly does work in unusual way. His ways are higher than ours. When God blesses us, He does so in a way that makes it unmistakable that He did it, and in a way that brings glory to Him. I know you're upset that you thought going to school and getting a degree was going to catapult you to success, but it didn't happen that way. You had to drop out of college due to financial and family difficulties and watch your dreams float off into the distance. I know you're upset that things didn't go as planned. That man you were engaged to, the one who seemed like Mr. Right, turned around and ripped your heart out of your chest by betraying you, or he passed away after an unexpected tragedy that left your head spinning. I know you're upset that God didn't stop the storms from arising and prevent pain from striking your heart through unexpected loss. I know you feel as if your life would be so much further ahead had you not made certain decisions and mistakes that set you back, dumping you in the place you're currently in. I know.

But like Joseph, the dungeon is exactly where you're supposed to be. That's where you're about to discover your true value and make Kingdom connections that are about to take you to the mountaintop. God doesn't need perfect conditions to do what He's going to do in your life. He doesn't need you to have a clean record. He doesn't need you to have all of your ducks in a row, have all of the tools man says you must have in order to succeed, have the favor of certain people. No! God loves to snatch the forgotten, the downcast, the overlooked, those who've been written off, those who don't have everything the world says we must have to succeed. God reaches down into the dungeons of life to grab the next world shaker. It's from the dungeons he grabbed people like Bishop T.D. Jakes and Joyce Meyers. It's from the dungeons He raises great and powerful men. In fact, while you're in the dungeon, that's when God speaks to you about the greatness that's inside of you. You see, the gift of God was in operation in Joseph while he was in the dungeon. The dream God gave Joseph was still burning in his soul while he was in the dungeon. Now, Joseph couldn't see how it was going to come to pass, but it was still there nonetheless.

Write out the vision God gives you while in the dungeon. Dream while in the dungeon. Begin to see yourself the way God sees you while you're in the dungeon. Why? Because if you wait until you're finally in the palace, it will be too late to step into your true identity then. God is preparing you for where He's taking you while you're in that dungeon situation. Stop complaining and start thanking Him. Lift your hands and tell the Lord yes, and let Him know you trust Him. You're at the right place at the right time.

I couldn't understand it. I couldn't understand why God wouldn't allow me to work a job, and why He wouldn't allow me to purchase my own place. He didn't want me to get settled. For had I gotten comfortable, I would have told God no and hunkered down. God knew me better than I knew myself. He had much for me to do, and He didn't want me to get tied down. He was sending me from place to place because there were people He meant for me to reach. It's funny that every house I'd housesit, the people I worked for would tell me how much I'd changed their lives and been a blessing to them. God was preaching to them through my life, through my character, through my deeds and actions. And yes, there were occasions where God opened doors for me to preach to them through my words.

Furthermore, God used that period in my life as another testament of His grace and goodness so that my experiences could preach to you. It wasn't enough for me to write a book and tell you how good God is, and simply tell you God can provide. God wanted me to use my testimony as the sermon. He wanted you to see His hand in my life and bear witness to how God moves, how He is able to bless us beyond our wildest imaginations.

God blessed me with several clients. There was one gentleman I went to work for, he fell upon sudden financial hardship due to a tax situation and couldn't pay me. But I continued to work for him. Eventually, things turned around for him and he paid me everything he owed me. And during the entire time I wasn't being paid, God still took care of my needs.

On another occasion, I was in California when I decided to stop by a facility I used to work at. The boss fired me several years prior. But now, I wanted to stop by to pay a few of the residents a visit just for old time's sake. When I knocked on the door, the very boss that fired me answered it. I was taken aback by the fact that he was still there. He recognized me and was pleasantly surprised to see me. His first words to me were, "Are you ready to return to work?"

What? This man must have lost his mind, I thought. He was the one who fired me a few years earlier. And now, he's begging me to come back and work for him? He begged and begged and begged. I kept telling him I had no intentions on staying, but he insisted that I come back to work for him. I finally caved in and went back to work for him. Again, I had a great place to stay and was receiving a handsome salary. God kept opening door after door after door for me. Not once did I have to beg God for money, beg God for a place to stay. The moment He told me to pack my things and put them into storage and step out in obedience to Him, the blessings began chasing me down, they began seeking me out. One person after another would call me out of the blue and offer me a place to stay and pay me for staying there.

Money stopped being an issue for me the second I obeyed God. Like David wrote, "I was young and now I am old, yet I have never seen the righteous forsaken or their children begging bread" (Psalm 37:25, NIV). David said never! The righteous are never abandoned by God and left to fend for themselves. The righteous never have to beg. In fact, their children never have to beg. The blessing of God is so big, it overflows from our lives to our children's lives. Even our grandchildren benefit from the blessing of God upon us. But we must learn to trust and obey Him. We must learn to drop our pride and allow Him to do things His way. That's why I want to take the next chapter and dive deep into the subject of walking by faith. God has so much in store for you. He sees the beginning from the end, and nothing catches Him by surprise. But to experience God's plan for you and walk in your calling, you must first learn how to walk by faith.

Chapter 5

WALKING BY FAITH

NOW THAT I THINK ABOUT IT, GOD blessed and prospered me financially because He wanted me to be in the position to live out my purpose and do His will without relying on any provisions from the church or anyone else. God did that. He opened doors for me outside of the church to prosper so that I wouldn't feel the need to compromise my faith and integrity just to make ends meet. What do I mean by that? Well, let me show you.

The Apostle Paul, in 1 Corinthians 9, explained what one of the biggest challenges facing many Christians, ministry leaders especially, is. He talked about money. He wrote,

"Don't you know that those who serve in the temple get their food from the temple, and that those who serve at the altar share in what is offered on the altar? In the same way, the Lord has commanded that those who preach the gospel should receive their living from the gospel." (vs. 13-14, NIV)

So the ministry is supposed to be a full-time thing, not a part-time gig. If we're called to preach the Gospel, whether as traveling evangelists or pastors, then we're supposed to devote all of our time and energy into doing just that. But as Paul explained in that chapter, sometimes this can be difficult, especially when people refuse to give to the work of the ministry.

In Paul's case, he faced a dilemma. See, he was an apostle—he traveled throughout Asia minor and Europe planting churches. This was hard work. He'd endured many obstacles along the way: being shipwrecked, nearly stoned to death, attacked on multiple occasions, attacked by wild animals, and even imprisoned. He went through it. But he endured. He kept going. He didn't allow anything to stop him. But there was one thing threatening to derail him: the lack of funding. It took money to do all of that traveling. It took money to eat, and to find a place to sleep at night. So Paul complained to the Church of Corinth about their lack of financial support. But then, he wrote something in that passage that ought to change your perspective on ministry forever. He wrote,

"But I keep under my body, and bring it into subjection: lest that by any means, when I have preached to others, I myself should be a castaway." (1 Corinthians 9:27)

The word "castaway" is translated adokimos in the Greek, and it means "reprobate". This is the same Greek word used in Romans 1:28 where Paul talked about God giving the sinners over to their sins because of the hardness of their hearts. Paul said God "gave them over to a reprobate mind, to do those things which are not convenient."

Paul's warning was firm. If we become greedy in heart and start preaching for money, if the ministry becomes all about getting prosperity, if we compromise the message of the Gospel in order to gain money and popularity, God will cast us aside as reprobates. The definition of the word reprobate is "not standing the test, not approved; unproved." So God will consider us to be unproven, incapable of handling His glory, incapable of handling favor, elevation, and more. We'll be deemed unusable. That's scary!

First, God will test your heart to see if you'll be willing to preach His Word "in season and out of season" (which means when it's convenient and when it's not convenient); and not only that, but preach the uncompromising Word even when people are against you and don't agree with a word you're saying. God will test your faithfulness. If you pass the test, He'll give you more. But He has to see your heart and commitment first.

When you prove your faithfulness to God, He'll open up doors for you financially so you can do His will without the burden of lack weighing you down.

That's important because most preachers and teachers water-down and compromise the message of the Gospel because they're weighed down by financial lack. So, rather than prove their faithfulness to God, they begin to appease people, forgetting that God is their true source.

God knew my heart. He tried me. Despite all of the pressures placed on me, I not once sought to preach a sinner-friendly, Christ-less Christianity where the cross is omitted and sin is excused. Furthermore, I refused to preach manmade traditions—I refused to bow to them and allow them to gag me. I never once made money an issue. My mission was deliverance. I wanted people to get free from religious bondage and spiritual deception. People knew me for that, and I was unapologetic in my approach and position.

I'd developed longevity in the spirit. I wasn't a novice, a fly-by-night or flash-in-the-pan who was looking for some fame and money. No, I was in it for the long-haul, my focus being on ministry as instructed in the Bible.

Paul warns us in 1 Timothy 3:6, "An elder must not be a new believer, because he might become proud, and the devil would cause him to fall" (NLT). When people jump up too quick and seek to be put in positions of leadership within the church, oftentimes they're not ready to lead. They haven't been tested and proven first. Even Jesus had to endure testing in the wilderness according to Matthew chapter four. And it is truly a test to remain faithful to God and do His will without compromise even when your lights are off, when you barely have any gas in your tank, when you barely have any food in your refrigerator, when you're struggling to make ends meet, and when people are talking about you and mistreating you. It's a test to keep serving God when Satan is making you an attractive and tempting offer, promising you that if you just change your message a little and make certain changes in your lifestyle, he'll hook you up with money and influence galore and you'll never have to worry about how you're going to pay your bills and feed your family. That's a tempting proposition, but every gift Satan gives us is gold-plated.

Stay faithful to God because He is faithful to His promises. He will provide for you even when things get rough. You may not be in that season of abundance yet. You might be in the wilderness season where God provides for you just enough manna to get by for that day, but if you pass this test, you'll soon find yourself in the Promised Land where provisions flow like a river. This is the place of abundance and overflow. Remember what Paul said in Galatians 6:9:

> "So let's not get tired of doing what is good. At just the right time we will reap a harvest of blessing if we don't give up." (NLT)

God blessed me financially in such a way that I didn't have to worry about money when it came to ministry. I had the freedom to do what He called me to do without having to wonder if I'd be able to support myself in the process. All I had to do was learn to walk by faith.

But what does that mean? We hear it all the time, but no one really explains it to us. So let's take these next two chapters and discuss what it actually means to walk by faith. Are you ready? I hope so.

WHAT IS FAITH?

First, we need to begin with a formal definition of faith. What is faith? Glad you asked. Faith is simply believing in and trusting God. Simple enough! Of course, we know people put faith in all kinds of things, but as followers of Christ, we place our faith in God—more specifically, the God of the Bible.

What does it really mean to trust God? It means to take Him at His Word. If He says He is going to do something, believe that He "is not a man that He should lie" (Numbers 23:19). God cannot lie. If He speaks something into the atmosphere, it must happen. If He were to say, "This sky is purple," the sky would suddenly become purple. And that's because, as John 1:3 says, everything that exists was created by God's Word. His Word has creative power— it creates! Whatever He speaks manifests.

Now, when it comes to us, God's Word becomes active in our lives when we believe it. When we take God's Word to heart and choose to believe it, the creative power of God's Word becomes active in our hearts and it produces what God said in our lives. That's why Jesus often referred to the Word of God as a seed. You plant a seed in your heart, and then it produces fruit over time. Sometimes the Word of God manifests in our lives instantly; sometimes it takes time. Just know that, like any seed, it grows when you plant it in the right soil.

Of course, I emphasize the right soil for a reason. Not every heart is good soil. Not every Believer... believes! There are those of us who quote the Word of God but doubt it will come to pass; that's the wrong soil. Also, there are those of us who speak the Word of God but have the wrong motives in our hearts; according to James 4:1-3, that's the wrong soil. Impure motives will render the seed useless. There are others of us who're trying to sow the seed of the Word in the soil of religion and manmade philosophy; according to Mark 7:13, that's the wrong soil. I cannot mix the Word of God with manmade philosophy and manmade religious beliefs and expect it to manifest in my life. God's Word must be pure in our hearts, free from worldly contaminates.

In Matthew 13:3-9, Jesus talked about the Parable of the Sower. He talked about having the right soil for the seed of the Word. He said,

> "He told many stories in the form of parables, such as this one: 'Listen! A farmer went out to plant some seeds. As he scattered them across his field, some seeds fell on a footpath, and the birds came and ate them. Other seeds fell on shallow soil with underlying rock. The seeds sprouted quickly because the soil was shallow. But the plants soon wilted under the hot sun, and since they didn't have deep roots, they died. Other

seeds fell among thorns that grew up and choked out the tender plants. Still other seeds fell on fertile soil, and they produced a crop that was thirty, sixty, and even a hundred times as much as had been planted! Anyone with ears to hear should listen and understand.'" (NLT)

Shallow soil. There, Jesus was referring to people who don't fully take the Word to heart. They let it sit on the surface level of their hearts but never allow it to take root inside of them. He was saying they were willing to believe God's Word when times where good, but were unwilling to hold on to their faith when times got hard. Trust when I tell you, your faith will get tested, and times will get difficult. But it's in those seasons you need to cling to your faith more tightly and don't let go. It's only a season and a test.

Rocky soil. That's soil that is too hard for the seed to penetrate. Simply put, there are some who're too resistant to God's Word. They refuse to budge, to give an inch and consider the possibility that God may be right and that His Word is telling the truth. The Word cannot manifest in that person's life.

Thorny soil. That's soil that has too many weeds in it; and by thorns and weeds, Jesus was referring to the cares of this world. In other words, when your allegiance and commitment is to the world rather than God, you'll prioritize the things of this world over God. When one allows their focus and attention to be stolen by the world, they're allowing weeds to creep into their hearts and choke the life out of the Word. They smother God in their hearts. They stamp out their faith.

Therefore, Jesus urges us to examine our hearts to make sure they're open to receive the truth, and that they're not committed and dedicated to the things of this world. Also, He urges us to make sure our hearts are willing to commit to His Word when times are good and bad.

*

Another critically important step in learning to walk by faith is monitoring who and what you listen to on a constant basis. We tend to forget that words are important. Like I mentioned just a second ago, words are seeds. Not only is God's Word a seed, but negative words also.

God wants to use us mightily, but many of us are limited in our thinking, which blocks what God is trying to do within us and through us. Remember the Israelites? I'm reminded of Numbers chapter thirteen where God commanded them to possess the Land of Canaan. They were excited about taking the land until the spies who scouted out the land came back with their report. They told everyone the land was beautiful and bountiful just as God described it, but that it also contained giants, the sons of Anak. And it was this statement that showed what their true problem was: "Next to them we felt like grasshoppers, and that's what they thought, too" (NLT).

The Israelites viewed themselves as grasshoppers, as insignificant and small compared to their enemies.

WHO SAID A WOMAN CAN'T PREACH?

And it was because of their poor self-image they refused to obey God and enter into the Promised Land. When we see ourselves the wrong way, we hinder the work of God in our lives. This is why it's important that you first take the time to study God's Word and learn what He thinks about you before attempting to step into your purpose. Discover your identity in Christ before you try to do anything for Him. Discover who you are so you can cast off false identities and ungodly expectations. That's the first discovery you need to make.

So many people want to do a great work for God without first taking the time to discover who they are in Christ, which is backwards. Before I could enter into the ministry, I had to take the time to discover who I was in Christ. This discovery gave me the courage to deal with the detractors who were waiting to hurl discouraging and hurtful words my way. Having an understanding of who I am in Christ prepared me for the "Women can't preach! Who do you think you are? You're out of line! Only a man is qualified to preach the Gospel" comments. I knew what God said about me. I knew that there is "neither male nor female" in Christ Jesus according to Galatians 3:28. I knew that God could use me just like He used Deborah, Phoebe, Pricilla, Mary and the other women in the Bible God used. I realized that gender isn't an issue with God when it comes to preaching, teaching, prophesying, praying, laying hands on the sick and all other works of the Kingdom. I realized the limitations being imposed on me were made by man, not God.

86

CHAPTER 5: WALKING BY FAITH

If you don't know who you are, you'll be easily misled.

Back to the Israelites. They had all the tools needed to defeat their enemies. Mainly, they had the biggest, most powerful weapon of all: God. God was on their side. God promised to be with them. God vowed to give them victory over the giants. What the Israelites forgot is it was always God who gave them victory over their enemies, and most of those enemies were too big and powerful for the Israelites. Think about it. God gave them victory over the Egyptians who were the biggest, most powerful military and economic force on the planet at the time. He also gave them victory over the City of Jericho, whose walls were impregnable. They forgot that the victories they'd received in the past came as a result of the supernatural power of God, not their ability and strength. Now, they were relying on their own strength and comparing their size to that of the giants who towered over them.

God will give you victories over situations that should crush you to teach you to how to trust in Him and not your own ability. We mess up when we look to our own abilities to make things happen for us. This is what God meant when he told Paul, "My grace is sufficient for you, for my power is made perfect in weakness" (2 Corinthians 12:9, NIV). When we are weak, God's strength kicks in. But when we rely on our strength, God backs away and allows us to do things on our own. And this is how we end up experiencing disaster.

God's will; God's bill. God provides where He

guides. If God gives you an assignment, He will send the provisions for the assignment ahead of time. He wants to be the one to make things happen in your life so that only He can get the credit. Remember, God blesses us for His glory and name's sake, not ours.

The biggest mistake the Israelites made in their journey to the Promised Land was listen to the spies' report, which God referred to as an "evil report" in Numbers 13:32. God punished the nation for listening to and believing this report, declaring,

> "How long shall I bear with this evil congregation, which murmur against me? I have heard the murmurings of the children of Israel, which they murmur against me. Say unto them, As truly as I live, saith the LORD, as ye have spoken in mine ears, so will I do to you: Your carcases shall fall in this wilderness; and all that were numbered of you, according to your whole number, from twenty years old and upward, which have murmured against me, doubtless ye shall not come into the land, concerning which I sware to make you dwell therein, save Caleb the son of Jephunneh, and Joshua the son of Nun. But your little ones, which ye said should be a prey, them will I bring in, and they shall know the land which ye have despised. But as for you, your carcases, they shall fall in this wilderness. And your children shall wander in the wilderness forty years, and bear your whoredoms, until your carcases

be wasted in the wilderness. After the number of the days in which ye searched the land, even forty days, each day for a year, shall ye bear your iniquities, even forty years, and ye shall know my breach of promise. I the LORD have said, I will surely do it unto all this evil congregation, that are gathered together against me: in this wilderness they shall be consumed, and there they shall die. And the men, which Moses sent to search the land, who returned, and made all the congregation to murmur against him, by bringing up a slander upon the land, Even those men that did bring up the evil report upon the land, died by the plague before the LORD. But Joshua the son of Nun, and Caleb the son of Jephunneh, which were of the men that went to search the land, lived still." (Numbers 14:27-38)

God punished the Israelites to dwell in the wilderness for forty years—one year for each day the spies were in the Promised Land. The punishment was severe because God had proven Himself over and over again to them, and yet, they still doubted Him.

Doubt and unbelief are dangerous things. It's because of unbelief that Jesus was unable to perform miracles in His hometown of Nazareth (Mark 6:5). The Bible says without faith it is impossible to please God (Hebrews 11:16). Also, God refers to unbelief as the product of an "evil heart" (Hebrews 3:12). But where does doubt and unbelief come from?

We begin to doubt God when we get around people who doubt God. This is a situation we've seen over and over again: a person loves and believes God, but then they get around other individuals who doubt God and His Word; they start listening to those individuals' words and arguments, and next, they begin doubting God. The company you keep is vitally important to your success, both spiritually and physically.

1 Corinthians 15:33 says, "Do not be deceived: 'Evil company corrupts good habits'" (NIV). When Paul says, "Do not be deceived," he was telling us not to fool ourselves into thinking we can hang around the wrong people and not be affected by their words and actions. It's impossible to remain in ungodly environments and not be negatively influenced by them. This is why the writer of Hebrews told, "And let us not neglect our meeting together, as some people do, but encourage one another, especially now that the day of his return is drawing near" (10:25, NIV). If we hang around people who encourage us in our faith and help us remain focused on the things of God, we'll be more inclined to honor and obey God when faced with challenging circumstances. But if we hang around people who sow the seeds of sin and doubt in our minds, those seeds will eventually take root and grow within us, and when the moment of testing arrives, we'll find ourselves acting out what we've been sowing in our hearts over time.

Another Scriptures explains it this way: "Do not be deceived: God cannot be mocked. A man reaps what he sows. Whoever sows to please their flesh, from the flesh will reap destruction; whoever sows to please the Spirit, from the Spirit will reap eternal life" (Galatians 6:7-8, NIV). The rule of nature is that you will reap what you sow. You can't sow apple seeds and reap oranges. You can't sow sinful and negative words and images into your heart and mind and reap righteous fruit (actions). You will live out the words and images you sow in your heart. If you look at pornography all day, you'll find yourself trying to live out what you see on the screen, and your relationships will suffer for it. If you listen to music filled with profanity and negative messages all day, you'll begin to think that way and seek to become what you hear in those songs. So God tells us to fix our attention on godly things (Colossians 3:2), and fill our hearts with His Word so we don't sin against Him (Psalm 119:11). The more we plant the Word of God in our hearts and minds by reading and meditating on it, the more we'll live it out and experience its benefits in our personal lives.

This is why you should stay in church—or at least, a God-fearing, Spirit-filled church. I know from experience that not all churches are the same; some don't teach and preach the Word of God. There are many churches that are what we call seeker-sensitive churches that preach a Christ-less Christianity. Some promote sin openly and even fly the rainbow colored flag proudly while trying to be accepted by an increasingly godless culture. These are the types of churches you want to avoid. However, there are plenty of good ones where the Word of God is being taught uncompromisingly. This is where you want to be. Why? Because it's in these environments you'll continually have the seed of the Word sown into your heart—and those seeds will eventually take root, sprout up and produce fruit.

Notice that fruit trees don't have to force fruit to grow; it just grows naturally. You don't have to force love, joy, peace, patience, kindness, goodness, faithfulness, gentleness, self-control (also known as The Fruit of the Spirit from Galatians 5:22-23) to develop in your life and take over your character; all you have to do is remain in an environment where the seeds of this fruit are being sown. Eventually, what you hear will rub off on you (influence you). So stay in the right environment if you want to walk by faith.

IT WAS A FAITH TEST

Believe this. There is a situation which will arise to provoke the believer into a thoughtful soul-searching faith evaluation. Any situation in life may be an occasion of temptation or testing but in it; there are a value, a quality, and an importance to your faith which must be considered because these very well may be the determining factors of the outcome. What is the extent or condition of your faith when tempted or tested? Regardless of how your evaluation tallies, The Lord is faithful. He will not allow the situation, temptation, trial, or test access beyond His word's ability and power to empower you to resist. He has told us in His word, "no test has come that the Lord has already given a means of escape that you may be capable and strong and powerful to bear up under it patiently (1Cor 10:13)." Believers cannot fall by a temptation if we cleave fast to the Lord by faith.

Scripture teaches what faith is, why faith, and how faith comes. "Now faith is the substance of things hoped for; the evidence of things not seen." Faith is powerful! It is the manifestation of our hopes and the proof though we cannot see it with our eyes. These things belong to heaven but God has given us his Spirit as a guarantee. We just have to trust God! Scripture also teaches "Without faith it is impossible to please God." This is so because faith is our access to the power of God and the access is NOW. So how does one obtain the faith to please God? Again, scripture teaches that "So then faith cometh by hearing, and hearing by the word of God." So it appears that the believer's faith is evaluated on how much they are listening to the preached words of Christ himself and how much they are hearing this good news of the gospel which results in faith. Also, faith comes because we have obeyed God's command of "not being conformed to this world, but transformed by the renewing of the mind (housed in the soul)." The renewed mind ingests the Word of faith that pleases God from the preaching of, and the studying of the word; for the sole purpose of the soul to hear and receive what's preached and studied and hiding it in the heart so to not sin against God through godless beliefs, thoughts, and actions. "For as he thinketh in his soul, so is he–(Darby Translation)." Only then the extent and condition of the believer's faith becomes like a spoken or written statement of their faith's true value, true quality, and true importance of effecting changed lives because of the living demonstration in trusting God as the way to go through a situation, trial, or test.

Have you ever been in a situation with no indication of how you got there? I'm talking about the situation that leaves life reeling in bewilderment. How? Why? Reading the word of God prepares all who has an ear to hear to walk by faith in these situations because without it, it is impossible to please God. Situations, tests, trials, and temptations are all synonymous in nature and to walk (our walk) is tantamount to how we live. But because of Jesus' obedience to redeem the fallen world on the cross at Calvary, the believer's obedience to live by faith, or trust in, or belief in Jesus and his perfectly finished work of redemption is the gateway to escape. This was planned by God for the believer when encountering the ruts and rocks in their path presenting those unrequested situations. Jesus even says explicitly that "I am the way, the truth and the life." Turn to Jesus and believe on him, for our life is a matter of faith. Our life is guided by faith not by what we can see. 2 Corinthians 5:7: "For we walk by faith, not by sight."

If you are a believer, you will learn to have complete trust in God. With this trust, the Holy Spirit (our heavenly helper in the earth) helps us rest in our belief that we have received what we hope for; cancelling any strategy of Satan to make us believe no proof is there at the beginning. Satan loves when believers think and believe with a carnal mind that the proof of trust or faith is evident in an outward appearance to the eyes after the test. It will be necessary to move even when you do not know where you are going when learning to have complete trust in God. If you have not read or heard this until now, let me assure you that evidence of your faith is there whether in God or a lie of the devil. Daily, the believer's walk of faith exhibits one or the other every moment. Whatever you do, do not allow fear to paralyze you. Fear is a ploy of the enemy of our souls, Satan, and he only comes to steal, kill, and destroy; planting fright, doubt, unbelief, worry, etc. to steal, kill, and destroy faith in God. Fear that disrupts our peace is demonic and cancels out faith in God. But belief in God and his word cancels out the demonic fear of Satan. We will operate in one or the other. Human faith is trusting in the Lord to work out every situation you find yourself in. If we want the faith of assurance in the Lord, live by a faith of adherence to obedience to God. When what we believe is evaluated, my advice is to always praise. For then the faith-in-God kind of answers come. Though not how we may have thought or when we may have desired. Many times we will feel as though God has turned a deaf ear. This is where the rubber meets the road. Why or how do answers come with praise? It is because of Jesus. An analysis of the 22nd Psalms informs us "God inhabitest, dwell in, dwellest amid, is seated among, and is enthroned on the praises of Israel." Israel is His covenant people and in the praise of his covenant people, he takes up residence. Now, because of Jesus, you and I are one of His covenant people. What a beautiful thought to remember in times of duress, distress, and despair! We have hope in Christ Jesus though tempted to complain.

As Christian believers often we forget that the Lord allows our steps in a situation because he wants to lead us where he wants us to go, teach us something we need to know, but always to something for our good. Let me share my testimony.

It was a Friday morning; I awakened in a panic. Fear had me paralyzed. All I could think was how bad the situation I was in. I had not a thought of how to process it either for I was totally apprehended.

Imagine your money being funny and your change being a little strange. This would not be so bad had I not been expecting my landlord to collect the rent. It was so frightening that I just lay in bed, not knowing what to do.

Suddenly it occurred to me that this is the day that the Lord has made, and I will rejoice and be glad in it! So I rebounded. I got up praising God and giving Him glory. The telephone rang.

You got it! It was the property owner calling to inform me that he was on the way to collect the rent. I said to him I'll be writing a check. To my astonishment he requested that I date it for the day when he could cash it. Pressured, I murmured to the Lord, "I do not even know what that date should be." That fast, a granule of faith arose and my heart and I knew what I do know; and that is there is the favor of God for the believer, Leander, His beloved. In my ministering, I have seen the mighty hand of God when the praises of believers go up. Many blessings have come down; some witnessed, some only reported.

Now I'm realizing that praise is where I should be focused, but I had allowed fear to obscure my faith. Focusing at this point in praise, all I'm thinking of is the goodness of God, what He has already done for me (even though there is still no finances available), and his promise to supply all (your) my need according to his riches in glory in Christ Jesus. I got favor from God right then, which no money can buy!

Not to mention there is the other bills due. Thank the Lord I am not consumed with that thought, and I have no concept of how to handle the situation!

It is now Saturday morning. I get up and off to prayer service I go. I returned home around 10 a.m. Shortly after I arrived a knock is on the door. To my surprise it was an old friend of mine. He had come from another city over an hour way. It had been a while since we had been in each other's company. Out of nowhere he said to me, Leander how is your financial situation? I felt ashamed and embarrassed. He is the last person who I would want to know the situation that I was in. I said to him, it is not something that I want to talk about. He looks at me in dismay and asked, "What do you mean you don't want to talk about it?" In return I asked what don't you understand. I do not want to talk about it. Then he said to me, "Well then, write it down."

As I began to write everything down, I discover that I had a total of $1164.00 in monthly expenses. The fear was overwhelming that morning; it had never occurred to me all that I needed. I just knew my situation was bad. I was not even aware it was to this degree.

Now that I am exposed, I see the total of my expenses and it brought me to tears.

Tears began to stream down my face. My friend asked, "Why are you crying"? I explained that I had no knowledge of how bad my situation was nor how to resolve that problem and it disturbed me. Now that I have it all before me, I need a substantial amount of money. He then said to me, that he would be able to help me. For the next time, we will have to figure out something. My thought was God forbid there is another time.

What was most astonishing is the fact that he was gathering information to see if my financial situation needed his support and not just probing.

He asks that I come and go with him to the credit union. He wanted to know if I would like cash or cashier's check. My thought is that cash would be best. I could deposit it in my checking account, and it would be available immediately. He went into the credit union to withdraw the money form his account. In my mind I tried to figure out what he may be able to help with now that there is a list of things to choose from. He returned to the car. Then he brought me to my bank. He gives me the money and I got out the car. I was going in the bank as I counted the money that I had just received from him. I counted twelve one hundred dollars bills. My tears are now of joy and astonishment. When I approached the teller, she could see I was crying. She asks why, and I told her someone had just given me this money. She said, "You must be a nice person deserving it." I let her know that I try to be. When I finished in the bank and returned to the car, my friend waiting, I let him know that I appreciated the relief with a thank you. He said to me don't thank me thank God!

It was at that moment that I realized that God had to lay on his heart my needs. No one else had knowledge of my situation. It became noticeably clear to me that day that if I trust God, He will take care of me. He knew how to uncover my needs to others whom he chooses despite the fact that my desire was not to share them.

The Lord sent my blessing, and my pride was trying to prevent me from receiving it. It was apparent to me that as a believer there is no need to beg, borrow, or steal. If by faith I trust God, He will provide all that I need. I know that the Lord will make away.

We will have to let go of the enemy's pride in order for the Lord to bless us.

WHO SAID A WOMAN CAN'T PREACH?

Chapter 6

HEARING THE VOICE OF GOD

THE NEXT THING YOU MUST LEARN TO DO IF you're going to walk by faith is listen to the voice of God. The Bible says, "For we walk by faith, not by sight" (2 Corinthians 5:7, NIV). As we established earlier, faith is defined as hearing and obeying the voice of God. God speaks; we listen and obey. God tells us to do something, we do it, plain and simple. Jesus said, "It is written: 'Man shall not live on bread alone, but on every word that comes from the mouth of God'" (Matthew 4:4, NIV). Words continually proceed from God's mouth, but are we listening? Do we know how to listen?

Well, if you're wrestling with this, let me help you out. Jesus gave us the Holy Spirit as a guide and teacher according to John 16:13. Ultimately, when we say we hear the voice of God, we're referring to the Holy Spirit speaking to us. But how does the Holy Spirit communicate with us? He speaks to our spirits according to Romans 8:16, which says, "For his Spirit joins with our spirit to affirm that we are God's children" (NLT). Basically, the Holy Spirit will whisper something into our hearts, and our spirits will bear witness to what the Holy Spirit is saying; it's sort of like an inner impression that's left on our spirits telling us what to say or do. And to further verify to us that He is the one speaking to us, the Holy Spirit will confirm His voice using God's Word, the Bible. He'll bring up a Bible verse in our minds that addresses exactly what we're dealing with at the moment. Furthermore, He will send people to confirm what He said to us—usually, prophetic confirmation. A prophet of God might speak to you concerning something you know God told you, thereby verifying to you that you truly heard God.

Yes, learning to hear the voice of the Holy Spirit takes practice. We have to learn to listen for that still small voice from within first and then match what we heard with that which is recorded in God's written word, the Bible. We have to pay close attention to those impressions we get in our hearts about certain people and situations. Some impressions are good, and some are bad. Regarding certain matters, after praying about them, we may feel a sense of peace, while a sense of dread may overcome us in others. Listen to your spirit; that's who the Holy Spirit is speaking to.

Now, I would love to spend more time elaborating on this, but perhaps I will dive deeper into this subject in another book. But for now, realize that these are sure ways God communicates with us. And I must note that God never communicates to us through things that are demonic: ouija boards, occult tools, astrology, horoscopes, psychics (who the Bible actually describes as operating under the power of a serpent spirit from Satan according to Acts 16:16, necromancy—speaking to the spirits of the dead, and more). God uses His Word, His ministers, and His Holy Spirit as His means of communicating with us.

KNOWING GOD'S VOICE

I'd awakened out of my sleep, out of what I thought to be nowhere. I then heard a voice say to me, "Call this friend and apologize." The friend was the guy I was in a relationship with when I accepted the call of God to the ministry. The guy promised to marry me, but he didn't want to accept the change in my life. So in an attempt to fix it, I moved to Georgia.

He came to Georgia where I lived at the time. Reconciling our relationship, we set in place the prerequisites for a wedding ceremony. We had our blood test done and secured our marriage license. Then another situation between us arose. This time, he told me he couldn't afford to get married.

He didn't want to change. Knowing I was in a relationship with God and that my life had changed, and by that, I'm referring to my lifestyle, I didn't want to do things the way we did them before. I was a new creation in Christ. But my fiance didn't understand that.

He left me to and went back to his home state. I

hadn't seen or heard from him in years. But I was so in love with the Lord, being single didn't bother me. I was busy focusing on the ministry.

I immediately apologised and repented to the Lord for not obeying His voice. I assured the Lord that He was the one I loved. I began offering praise and worship to the Lord. I felt assured by the Spirit of God that I was living my new life in Christ, and He was all I needed. My praise and worship continue to be fortified with prayer. However, another situation developed in my relationship with Christ. I couldn't understand why I was thinking about this man, whom I had not seen nor heard from in years, at this place and time. Why was I thinking about him, especially as I was waking up? I felt like the devil was trying to distract me from my relationship with God.

I kept apologizing to the Lord and telling Him I loved Him. I began quoting scriptures, making them personal. "Lord, you are why I live, move, and have my being. You are Lord; I am your offspring" (Acts 17:28). You are everything to me: my intellect, the reason I exist, the source of my actions and thoughts. You are omnipresent. My focus on Scripture made it clear that I heard the voice of the Lord.

*

It was about midday when I heard, " When has the devil ever told anyone to apologize?" I felt appalled for allowing the deceiver to prolong my obedience to the Lord.

The enemy's goal is to steal, kill and destroy. For

sure, I got blindsided by his deception. It's not surprising because he is who he is and is doing what he does. Scripture confirms this: "The thief cometh not, but for to steal, and to kill and to destroy; I am come that they may have life, and that they might have it more abundantly." (John 10:10 KJV)

Now I understand better why the Lord tells us to cast all our cares on Him and be sober-minded. "Be sober, be vigilant: for your adversary the devil, as a roaring lion, walks about seeking whom he may devour" (1 Peter 5:6 KJV). A relationship with God is the key to appropriating God's promises.

My relationship with the Lord gives me a desire to please him. When we establish a relationship with God, it becomes easy to keep His commandments. We are born in sin. The law is unnecessary now that I am born again (saved by faith). I have a relationship with Jesus Christ because of His shed blood. I have been set free! I am justified by grace through faith. Justification makes a sinner righteous before God. The righteousness of Christ in me seeks to please Him through me. Scripture confirms this: Romans 1:5-6 says, "By whom we have received grace and apostleship, for obedience to the faith among all nations, for his name: Among whom are ye also the called of Jesus Christ." Also, Romans 10:4 says, "Christ is the end of the law for righteousness to everyone that believeth. Jesus came that we have abundant life."

It has been a few years since my relationship with the guy I thought would marry me ended. Reflecting back, God was instructing me, "Call this friend and apologize." God also told me what to say. I had to submit to what God wanted rather than what I wanted. So, I prepared myself and made the telephone call.

He answered. Immediately, I said, "I just called to apologize."

"Apologize," he responded, shocked. "Apologize? I probably owe you an apology. You apologize for what?"

"I am apologizing because I feel like you abandoned and deceived me and you stopped all communication."

"Sounds like I owe you an apology. You need to come here so we can talk."

"If we need to talk, you should come here."

"That's no problem," he replied. Then he promised to visit and said he would be there in a couple of days. I agreed to the visit and ended the call.

After that, I felt the need to go on a three-day fast. I started my fast the very next day. Before daybreak, the morning of the second day of my fast, I thought the Lord told me that man was my husband. So, I completed the fast and awaited his arrival excitedly, believing I'd heard God concerning us. But did I hear God? Again, the devil is very deceptive. Sometimes, he'll play on our emotions and fleshly desires and get our hopes up concerning things we won't rather than things God wants for us. A little leaven will ruin the whole lump, as Jesus said - the leaven of deception. I wasn't moving in the will of God; I was only acting on what my flesh desired and calling it God.

CHAPTER 6: HEARING THE VOICE OF GOD

When he arrived, I met him at the bus station. I decided it was okay for him to stay at my house. We woke up the next morning, had breakfast, and went to church. In those days, Sunday school began at 9:30 A.M., and church lasted from 11 A.M. until around 2 P.M. Then the night service started at about six or seven o'clock and continued until the Holy Spirit released us. I'm all in. All-day service is all right with me. I'm in love with the Lord. But my partner didn't have the same passion. So, he decided not to attend the night service. He stayed home. He said, "I will be here when you get back." As I was en route to church, it occurred to me that we had not talked about anything concerning the reason for his visitation. He didn't address why he was there and what he wanted from me or for the two of us. But I just overlooked that, believing that I heard God concerning the two of us, thinking he was my husband.

*

When I returned home, he was on the sofa watching the game. I called it a night and went to bed. As I lay there, I felt the urge to take him to a friend of mine who was a Clinician with an earned Doctorate Degree and introduce him to her. Her clinic was within walking distance. I reached out to her to see if it was alright that we stop by, and she said yes.

The following day, he got up, and I told him I had someone I would like him to meet. He agreed, and we were on our way. Once we arrived, my girlfriend greeted us. She is an anointed sister who walks in her God-given calling. From the start, her conversation with us focused on every issue on our agenda without me having to tell her anything that was happening. Of course, my partner was trying to avoid the conversation. He seemed hesitant to discuss anything concerning our "relationship". He appeared to have hidden intentions. On the way back home, I confronted him about being a con. He denied being a con but agreed he had "been there and done that" in the past.

When I arrived back at the house, two of my best friends were there, one of whom was a preacher. This was a surprise because I was not sure why they were there. I thought to myself, we can get married. After all, the Lord did confirm this is my husband, and these two will keep the secret until I am ready to announce it.

Both the preacher and I were associate ministers under the same Pastor. I didn't want to consult the pastor. For some reason, I was nervous about bringing the matter of marriage to him. Of course, this only made the situation even more complicated. In hindsight, the encounter with my clinician friend was more than just a visit; it was a red flag God was giving me about the man I was involved with. But I was not listening to the Spirit of God in my heart. Instead, I was listening to my flesh.

*

In conclusion, I resolved that all things work together for good to those who love God and are called according to His purpose (Romans 8:28). Mind transformation!

At this point, he left the very next day to return

to his hometown. I didn't give it another thought and continued life as usual.

A few days later, I got up to start my day as usual. As I entered the bathroom, I heard the Lord say, "Pack your bag and go to California." I thought, California? Then I heard the Lord speak into my heart, "That man was who you wanted, but being that I have chosen you, know that I have greater in store for you. Eyes have not seen, ears heard, nor has it entered the mind the things I have prepared for those who love me" (1 Corinthians 2:9 KJV).

As you read this testimony, know that the Lord is faithful. If He said it, He'll perform it. Trust God's voice even when it makes no sense.

*

"When I learned how to walk by faith, my life changed. I discovered I had a constant guide and companion to lead me through life's toughest circumstances. I discovered that this is the true path to victory in life. We're not supposed to live our lives in a state of fear, confusion, and uncertainty. The Bible says, "It is useless for you to work so hard from early morning until late at night, anxiously working for food to eat; for God gives rest to his loved ones" (Psalm 127:2, NLT). Rest is so valuable, so important. Some people have millions of dollars in the bank but can't find a moment of rest. And it's not because they don't have the money to take luxury vacations. They can. They can fly worldwide, book rooms in the most expensive hotels and resorts, jump on yachts and private jets, and more. And yet, their minds are inundated with fear, worry, anxiety, depression, confusion, and defeatism. Some of these individuals, you may have seen or heard of. They try to drown their sorrows in rivers of alcohol, choke them in clouds of smoke, bury them under avalanches of cocaine and other harmful substances, dance away their demons in the clubs, and distract themselves from their issues using promiscuous sex and other vices. They usually end up ending their careers and lives tragically; this is because money can't buy you peace. Peace doesn't come from people and material things; it comes from the presence of God, from knowing God's purpose for your life and allowing Him to fill your heart with His love and truth.

Jesus is called the Prince of Peace in Isaiah 9:6. He told us, "I am leaving you with a gift—peace of mind and heart. And the peace I give is a gift the world cannot give. So don't be troubled or afraid" (John 14:27, NLT). Peace is a gift only God can give; it's a supernatural one. You can't get this peace through transcendental meditation and yoga, through drugs and alcohol, through sex, through material things and worldly accomplishments; this peace is only provided to you through a relationship with God. It's His gift when you follow and trust Him with your life. And that's the key: you must trust Him with your life. That means give up all for Him and follow His path for you. His plans for you are better than your plans for yourself. His ways are higher than your ways. When He leads you, you experience so much more than just material blessings; you experience the ultimate fulfillment every person longs to experience. This is where you prosper physically, mentally, and emotionally." Let's pray:

> Dear Heavenly Father, I thank you for your presence in my life. Thank you for your Son, Jesus, the Christ, who shed His blood on the cross for my sins and rose from the grave on the third day. Today, I surrender my life to you. I thank you for washing me with the blood of Jesus so that I may be clean in your sight. I thank you for redeeming me and giving me abundant life. Thank you for making me a brand new creation in Christ. I am free from the hand of the enemy. I denounce the world. I also abandon my plans for your plans, for your will concerning me. Today, I receive your will for my life. Let your Kingdom come, and your will be done in my life. Holy Spirit, open my spiritual eyes. Let me see the enemy's strongholds on my heart and mind. Today, I come out of agreement with every lie of Satan concerning my life and identity. I know who I am in Christ Jesus. Today, I cast down every thought and imagination the enemy has planted in my heart and cast off every limitation the enemy has placed on me through deception. Holy Spirit, train my ears to hear and recognize your voice, for I want to walk according to your will. Today, I thank you for this and for doing a new work within me. In Jesus name, I pray, amen.

ABOUT THE AUTHOR

Leander Hicks is a licensed and ordained Christian minister. She has spent many years in ministry, serving in various capacities. She is the CEO & President at Alpha & Omega of GA Inc. She studied Organizational leadership at Biola University.

To contact the author, go to
abrilliantgem@aol.com

Printed in the USA
CPSIA information can be obtained
at www.ICGtesting.com
CBHW020051060924
13931CB00043B/734